CONTENTS

PREFACE

Unlocking the Gates of Laziness

Welcome, dear reader, to the whimsical world of laziness and wealth. As you embark on this delightful journey, allow me to set the stage and paint a vivid picture of what awaits you within the pages of this extraordinary tome.

In this preface, we shall explore the essence of laziness and its often-misunderstood relationship with financial success. We shall delve into the magical realm of lazy millionaires, where the pursuit of wealth is accompanied by a symphony of laughter and leisure. So, grab a cozy chair, put your feet up, and let us embark on this enchanting adventure together.

I. The Myth of Hard Work and the Rise of Laziness

Ah, the myth of hard work, a tale passed down through generations like a worn-out pair of work boots. Society has long glorified the virtues of toil, praising the sweat-soaked brows and calloused hands of those who burn the midnight oil. But dear reader, let me share a secret with you: the path to wealth need not be paved with endless labor.

As the brilliant inventor Thomas Edison once quipped, "Opportunity is missed by most people because it is dressed in overalls and looks like work." We must recognize that laziness is not the enemy; it is the catalyst for innovation and efficiency. Some of the greatest inventions and breakthroughs in history were born from the desire to simplify tasks and free up time for leisure.

Take, for example, the story of Henry Ford, the pioneering automobile magnate. Ford's lazy aversion to manual labor led him to revolutionize the assembly line, streamlining the production process and making automobiles accessible to the masses. His laziness was the spark that ignited a fiery trail of success.

II. The Lazy Millionaire's Manifesto: Leisure as a Pathway to Wealth

Now, my dear reader, let us dive into the heart of this manifesto —a celebration of leisure as the secret pathway to unimaginable wealth. The lazy millionaire's creed is simple: work smart, not hard. We reject the notion that success requires endless hours of tireless effort and sacrifice. Instead, we embrace a philosophy that champions efficiency, delegation, and the pursuit of passion.

As the wise Warren Buffett once said, "I always knew I was going to be rich. I don't think I ever doubted it for a minute." Buffett understood that wealth could be attained through strategic decision-making and focused effort, not by burning the midnight oil.

III. The Lazy Millionaires of Legend: Tales of Leisure and Success

Ah, let us regale ourselves with the tales of lazy millionaires who have etched their names into the annals of history. From the eccentric Howard Hughes, who amassed a fortune while indulging in his aviation and film passions, to the irreverent Richard Branson, who built a business empire while basking in the sun on his private island.

But it is not only the famous who have embraced the path of laziness. Countless everyday individuals have unlocked the gates of wealth by prioritizing leisure and leveraging their unique talents. Consider the story of Jane, a self-proclaimed "lazy entrepreneur" who turned her love for baking into a thriving online bakery, all while savoring the pleasure of lazy afternoons in her kitchen.

And so, dear reader, as you embark on this grand adventure, remember the words of the great playwright Oscar Wilde: "I choose my friends for their good looks, my acquaintances for their good characters, and my enemies for their intellects. A man cannot be too careful in his choice of enemies." Similarly, in your pursuit of wealth and laziness, choose your role models wisely, surround yourself with like-minded individuals, and let the naysayers marvel at your audacious laziness.

In Conclusion

As the preface draws to a close, I invite you, dear reader, to immerse yourself in the captivating chapters that lie ahead. Together, we shall unravel the mysteries of laziness and wealth, discover the art of efficient decision-making, and embrace a lifestyle that prioritizes leisure without compromising success.

Prepare yourself for a whimsical journey filled with laughter, inspiration, and practical wisdom. As you turn each page, remember the immortal words of the charismatic Mae West: "I never said it would be easy, I only said it would be worth it." And indeed, the lazy millionaire's path is worth every indulgent moment.

So, my dear companion, let us venture forth into the realms of laziness and wealth, hand in hand, ready to unlock the gates that lead to a life of abundance and leisure. The adventure awaits, and the journey promises to be nothing short of extraordinary. Let us begin!

ABOUT THE AUTHOR TONY TUSHAR POPAT - THE LAZY MAESTRO OF WEALTH AND WIT

Welcome, dear reader, to the remarkable world of Tony Tushar Popat, the indomitable force behind this book of laziness and financial success. In this chapter, we shall delve into the enigmatic persona of our beloved author, uncovering the secrets of his lazy genius and exploring the path that led him to become the maestro of wealth and wit.

I. The Rise of Tony Tushar Popat: From Couch Potato to Financial Extraordinaire

Ah, the tale of Tony Tushar Popat is a story that will leave you spellbound. Born with a natural aversion to hard work, young Tony was often found lounging on his favorite couch, dreaming of a life filled with leisure and abundance. Little did he know that this seemingly idle pursuit would become the cornerstone of his extraordinary journey.

As Tony grew older, he realized that the traditional path to success was not for him. He refused to conform to societal norms that dictated endless hours of labor and sacrifice. Instead, he harnessed his innate laziness and channeled it into a brilliant strategy for financial success.

II. The Lazy Maestro's Secrets: Unleashing the Power of Laziness

Tony Tushar Popat, the lazy maestro himself, understood that laziness was not a weakness to be overcome but a hidden strength waiting to be unleashed. He developed a unique framework that combined wit, strategic thinking, and the art of delegation to build his empire of wealth.

In the words of the great Albert Einstein, "I have no special talent. I am only passionately curious." Tony's curiosity became the catalyst for his success, driving him to explore unconventional paths, question the status quo, and seek out opportunities that aligned with his lazy ambitions.

III. The Lazy Maestro's Legacy: Inspiring Laziness for Generations to Come

Tony Tushar Popat's influence extends far beyond the pages of this book. He has become a beacon of inspiration for lazy dreamers and ambitious underachievers alike. His message of embracing laziness as a pathway to financial success has resonated with people around the world.

One of Tony's most cherished beliefs is that laughter is the key to a life well-lived. He often quotes the legendary Charlie Chaplin, who said, "A day without laughter is a day wasted." Tony understands the power of humor to uplift spirits, foster creativity, and create meaningful connections.

In Conclusion

As we bid adieu to this chapter, we have but scratched the surface of the enigmatic Tony Tushar Popat. Throughout this book, you will witness his wit, wisdom, and unwavering dedication to the pursuit of laziness. Brace yourself for an adventure unlike any other—a journey that will make you laugh, think, and question the conventional notions of success.

Tony Tushar Popat invites you to join him on this grand escapade into the world of lazy millionaires, where laughter and leisure intertwine with financial abundance. So, buckle up, dear reader, for the ride of a lifetime. As Tony himself would say, "Life is too short to work hard. Let's embrace laziness and unlock the gates to wealth and happiness together!"

And now, with a mischievous grin, Tony bids you adieu until we meet again in the next chapter. Until then, may your days be filled with laughter, your dreams be fueled by laziness, and your pockets be lined with the sweet fruits of your ingenious pursuits. Onward, my friend, to the lazy land of riches!

CHAPTER 1: INTRODUCTION

Welcome, fellow aspiring lazy millionaires! Prepare to enter a world where financial abundance and laziness go hand in hand. In this captivating chapter, we're about to shatter the age-old myth that hard work is the sole path to success. Get ready to embrace the concept of being a lazy millionaire and unlock the secrets to achieving financial freedom with minimal effort.

Now, some may raise an eyebrow at the idea of laziness being the key to success. After all, we've been conditioned to believe that hard work is the only respectable way to achieve our goals. But fear not, my friends, for we are about to embark on a journey that challenges the status quo and turns conventional wisdom on its head.

Imagine a life where you can lounge in luxury, sip on a refreshing drink, and watch your bank account flourish without breaking a sweat. Sounds too good to be true, doesn't it? Well, get ready to flip the script and make this dream a reality.

Our adventure begins by setting our sights on the ultimate goal: financial freedom. But here's the twist - we'll achieve it with minimal effort. Say goodbye to the grueling hours and the perpetual hustle. We are about to discover a smarter, more efficient approach to wealth-building.

But before we dive into the practical strategies and techniques, let's take a moment to debunk the myth that has held us captive for far too long - the belief that hard work is the only path to success. Sure, hard work has its place, but we're here to explore alternative paths to financial abundance.

Throughout the pages of this book, we will peel back the layers of hard work propaganda and reveal the exciting possibilities that come with being a lazy millionaire. We will delve into the art of delegation, outsourcing, and leveraging the expertise of others. It's time to bid farewell to the shackles of unnecessary toil and embrace a life where decision-making takes center stage.

So, fasten your seatbelts, my fellow lazy millionaires, because we're about to embark on a journey that will challenge your beliefs, ignite your imagination, and revolutionize your approach to wealth-building. Prepare to unleash your inner lazy genius as we rewrite the rules of success, one witty chapter at a time!

Now that you have a taste of what lies ahead, let's dive into the subsequent chapters and uncover the secrets to becoming a lazy millionaire. Get ready for an exhilarating ride filled with laughter, wit, and unconventional wisdom. Together, we will discover the art of laziness and turn it into a powerful tool for achieving financial freedom. Are you ready? Let's do this!

Welcome to the realm of the lazy millionaire mindset, where we'll uncover the secrets to achieving financial abundance with minimal effort. In this chapter, we'll explore the transformative power of shifting your mindset, embracing efficiency, and harnessing the incredible advantages of delegation and outsourcing. Prepare to challenge societal beliefs about hard work and laziness as we embark on this exhilarating journey together.

To begin our quest, we must first address the very foundation of our approach to success - our mindset. It's time to break free from the shackles of conventional thinking and adopt a new perspective that prioritizes efficiency and leverage. This isn't about being lazy in the traditional sense; it's about working smarter, not harder.

Imagine a world where your time is spent on strategic decision-making and high-level thinking, while the day-to-day tasks are effortlessly handled by others. That's the essence of the lazy millionaire mindset. By shifting our focus from doing everything ourselves to leveraging the skills and expertise of others, we unlock a new level of productivity and success.

One of the key pillars of the lazy millionaire mindset is the art of delegation. It's time to let go of the belief that we must do everything ourselves. Instead, we'll learn how to identify our strengths and weaknesses, and delegate tasks that fall outside our expertise. By entrusting competent individuals or outsourcing to skilled professionals, we not only lighten our workload but also tap into the power of specialization.

Outsourcing is another game-changing tool in the lazy millionaire's arsenal. It allows us to delegate tasks that are time-consuming or require specific expertise, freeing up our valuable time to focus on more critical aspects of our wealth-building journey. Whether it's hiring virtual assistants, engaging freelancers, or partnering with specialized agencies, outsourcing provides us with the ability to scale our efforts and achieve greater efficiency.

Now, let's address the elephant in the room - the societal beliefs that equate hard work with virtue and laziness with failure. We've been conditioned to believe that success can only be achieved through blood, sweat, and tears. But here's the secret: it's not about the amount of work we put in; it's about the quality of work and the strategic decisions we make.

By challenging these societal norms, we liberate ourselves from the burdensome expectations of non-stop hustle. We reclaim our right to enjoy the fruits of our labor and create a life where leisure and productivity coexist harmoniously. It's time to rewrite the narrative and embrace the truth that laziness, when approached intelligently, can be a powerful catalyst for success.

As we conclude this chapter, I urge you to reflect on your current mindset and consider the possibilities that lie ahead. By shifting your perspective, embracing efficiency, and leveraging the power of delegation and outsourcing, you'll lay the foundation for a lazy millionaire lifestyle that brings both financial abundance and a sense of freedom.

In the next chapter, we'll delve into specific strategies and techniques to outsource and delegate effectively, allowing you to maximize your time and effort. Get ready to witness the true magic of the lazy millionaire approach as we unveil the secrets to working smarter, not harder. Are you ready to embark on this exciting journey? Let's dive in and discover the art of laziness in all its glory!

CHAPTER 2: THE LAZY MILLIONAIRE MINDSET

Welcome, my fellow enthusiasts of leisurely affluence, to the captivating realm of the lazy millionaire mindset! In this chapter, we embark on an exhilarating journey that will unveil the secrets to achieving unparalleled wealth with the utmost ease. Get ready to challenge societal norms, redefine success, and embrace the transformative power of shifting your mindset towards efficiency, leverage, delegation, and outsourcing. Prepare yourself for a wild ride of wit, wisdom, and wealth-building wizardry!

Now, close your eyes and envision a life where you effortlessly navigate the realms of financial abundance. Imagine yourself reclining on a lavish yacht, basking in the sun's warm embrace, while sipping on a fruity cocktail. As you gaze out at the shimmering azure sea, you realize that this idyllic scene is not reserved for the "hard-working" alone. No, my friends, the lazy millionaire mindset is all about working smarter, not harder. It's about unlocking the door to opulence through strategic decision-making, calculated effort, and ingenious delegation.

But how do we break free from the chains of conventional thinking and embrace this audacious mindset? Well, it all starts with debunking the antiquated notion that success is solely measured by the hours we toil. In the grand tapestry of wealth creation, time is a precious resource, and it is our duty to wield it with skillful precision. The lazy millionaire mindset challenges the notion that busyness equates to productivity. Instead, it compels us to prioritize tasks that generate the highest value, while deftly delegating or outsourcing the rest.

Ah, delegation—a veritable superpower in the arsenal of the lazy millionaire! Imagine having a team of competent individuals who thrive on tackling the nitty-gritty tasks while you focus on the big picture. Delegation is the art of recognizing your strengths and weaknesses, identifying which tasks align with your core competencies, and entrusting the others to capable hands. It's about building a team of rock stars who share your vision and bring their unique expertise to the table.

Take the tale of Timothy, an enterprising entrepreneur with a penchant for laziness. While he possesses an innate knack for numbers and financial wizardry, he knows that graphic design is not his strong suit. So, Timothy deftly delegates the task of creating eye-catching marketing collateral to a talented graphic designer named Gina. This not only frees up his time to focus on making strategic business decisions, but it also ensures that his brand exudes an aesthetic appeal that captivates potential clients. Timothy becomes a true lazy millionaire by leveraging the talents of others to propel his business to dizzying heights.

But delegation is only part of the equation. Let us now venture into the enchanting world of outsourcing, where true magic awaits. Imagine having access to an extensive network of professionals who can handle specialized tasks with utmost expertise. Outsourcing allows us to tap into the collective brilliance of individuals who are dedicated to their craft, be it web development, content creation, or marketing strategy.

Imagine the tale of Isabella, a tenacious entrepreneur with dreams of conquering the online marketplace. She realizes that building a cutting-edge website is crucial to her success, but her coding skills are more akin to a dancing hippopotamus than a tech genius. In a stroke of brilliance, Isabella outsources the website development to a team of skilled developers who bring her vision to life. This not only saves her valuable time and frustration but also ensures that her online presence is nothing short of spectacular. Isabella waltzes her way to lazy millionaire status by leveraging the talents of outsourced experts.

Now, let us address the elephant in the room—the deeply ingrained societal beliefs that glorify hard work and vilify laziness. We've been conditioned to believe that success can only be achieved through ceaseless toil, sacrificing leisure, and living on caffeine drips. But here's a secret for you: the lazy millionaire mindset challenges these preconceived notions, liberating us from the clutches of burnout and allowing us to thrive in a harmonious balance of work and play.

In the words of the illustrious Mark Twain, "Work smarter, not harder." The lazy millionaire understands that it's not about the number of hours we put in; it's about the quality of our efforts. It's about making strategic decisions, seizing opportunities, and maximizing our impact. By rejecting the traditional definition of hard work and embracing the art of laziness, we pave the way for a life of fulfillment, abundance, and joy.

As we conclude this chapter, take a moment to reflect on your current mindset. Can you envision the possibilities that lie before you? By shifting your perspective and fully embracing the lazy millionaire mindset, you unlock the potential for a life of unparalleled prosperity and freedom. In the next chapter, we'll delve deeper into the specific strategies and techniques to outsource and delegate effectively, unraveling the full potential of your lazy millionaire journey.

So, my fellow seekers of wealth and leisure, are you ready to witness the true magic of the lazy millionaire mindset? Buckle up, as we embark on an extraordinary adventure that will transform the way you approach wealth creation. The path to becoming a lazy millionaire is right at your fingertips. Let's dive in and discover the art of laziness in all its glorious splendor!

CHAPTER 3: CREATING A VISION

Welcome, dear readers, to the exhilarating realm of creating a vision—an essential step on the path to lazy millionaire status. In this captivating chapter, we will explore the art of developing a clear vision of your desired lifestyle and financial goals. We will delve into the profound concept of aligning your passions with your wealth-building strategy and harnessing the power of visualization to bring your dreams to life. So, fasten your seatbelts and prepare to embark on a journey of self-discovery and boundless imagination.

Imagine yourself basking on a sun-kissed beach, sipping a refreshing beverage, and reveling in the joy of financial freedom. Now, hold on to that image, for it is the beginning of your journey toward becoming a lazy millionaire. Developing a clear vision is like drawing a treasure map that guides you through the twists and turns of your wealth-building expedition. As the visionary Walt Disney once said, "If you can dream it, you can do it." Let us dive into the process of crafting a compelling vision that will ignite your passion and steer you towards your lazy millionaire aspirations.

The first step in creating a vision is to take a moment to reflect on your desired lifestyle. Close your eyes and envision the life you wish to lead—a life of abundance, leisure, and fulfillment. What does it look like? How do you spend your days? What activities bring you the most joy? Embrace your imagination and let it run wild. Whether it's traveling the world, pursuing a hobby, or spending quality time with loved ones, allow your vision to encompass every aspect of the life you desire.

Once you have a vivid picture of your ideal lifestyle, it's time to align it with your financial goals. Remember, lazy millionaires are not just about lounging around; they are strategic in their pursuit of wealth and freedom. Take a moment to consider your financial aspirations. How much passive income do you wish to generate? What investments or businesses align with your passions? By identifying the financial milestones you want to achieve, you can begin to map out a path that leads to both financial success and the freedom to enjoy the lazy millionaire lifestyle.

Now, let's explore the magic of aligning your passions with your wealth-building strategy. Ask yourself, "What am I truly passionate about?" Passion is the fuel that drives lazy millionaires to great heights. It ignites the fire within, propelling you forward even when faced with challenges. Your passions can guide you toward wealth-building opportunities that not only generate income but also bring you joy and fulfillment. Consider the story of Julia, a passionate food enthusiast who turned her love for cooking into a thriving online cooking course business. By aligning her passion with her wealth-building strategy, Julia not only achieved financial success but also found deep satisfaction in sharing her culinary expertise with others. Remember, when you align your passions with your wealth-building journey, work becomes a source of joy rather than a chore.

Now, close your eyes once again and let's dive into the fascinating world of visualization. Visualization is a powerful tool that allows us to manifest our dreams into reality. As the renowned author Napoleon Hill once said, "Whatever the mind can conceive and believe, it can achieve." Take a few moments each day to visualize yourself living the life of a lazy millionaire. See yourself making strategic decisions, delegating tasks to a capable team, and enjoying the fruits of your labor. Visualize the abundance, the freedom, and the joy that comes with financial success. By consistently visualizing your desired outcomes, you are programming your subconscious mind to seek opportunities and take actions that will bring your vision to life.

To further illustrate the power of visualization, let's look at the story of Michael Phelps, the legendary Olympic swimmer. Throughout his career, Phelps used visualization techniques to mentally rehearse his races. He would imagine himself gliding effortlessly through the water, outpacing his competitors, and touching the wall first. By vividly visualizing success, Phelps harnessed the power of his mind and set numerous world records. His story is a testament to the transformative impact of visualization and the immense power it holds in shaping our reality.

As we conclude this chapter, I encourage you to embrace the creative process of creating a vision. Allow yourself to dream big, align your passions with your wealth-building strategy, and visualize your success with unwavering clarity. Remember, the lazy millionaire mindset is fueled by a powerful vision that acts as a compass, guiding you toward your desired destination.

So, my fellow dreamers, let us heed the wisdom of visionaries and thought leaders who have transformed their dreams into reality. As the iconic Steve Jobs once said, "Your work is going to fill a large part of your life, and the only way to be truly satisfied is to do what you believe is great work." Create your vision, believe in it wholeheartedly, and embark on the extraordinary journey to lazy millionaire status. The possibilities are limitless, and the rewards are beyond your wildest imagination. Let us continue our quest together, harnessing the power of visualization, and shaping our destinies with purpose and passion.

CHAPTER 4:
LEVERAGING
PASSIVE INCOME

Welcome, dear readers, to the exciting realm of passive income —the golden ticket to lazy millionaire status. In this captivating chapter, we will explore the art of leveraging passive income to build wealth effortlessly. We will embark on a journey through various sources of passive income, including dividend stocks, real estate, and other income-generating assets. So, sit back, relax, and prepare to discover the secrets of generating income while you sleep.

Passive income is the holy grail of lazy millionaires—it is income earned with minimal effort and little to no active involvement. Unlike traditional earned income, which requires continuous time and effort, passive income streams continue to flow even when you're not actively working. As the brilliant Warren Buffett once said, "If you don't find a way to make money while you sleep, you will work until you die." Let us explore the avenues that can lead us to financial freedom and a life of leisure.

One of the most popular sources of passive income is through dividend stocks. Dividend stocks are shares of companies that distribute a portion of their earnings to shareholders in the form of dividends. By investing in dividend-paying companies, you become a partial owner and can enjoy a regular stream of passive income. The beauty of dividend stocks lies in their ability to generate income regardless of market conditions. Even during downturns, reputable dividend-paying companies continue to distribute dividends, providing a stable income stream. As the wise Benjamin Graham once said, "The true investor...will do better if he forgets about the stock market and pays attention to his dividend returns and to the operating results of his companies."

Real estate is another lucrative avenue for passive income. By investing in rental properties, you can generate consistent cash flow through monthly rental income. Imagine owning a portfolio of properties that work tirelessly to generate income while you focus on other endeavors. Rental properties not only provide a steady stream of passive income but also offer the potential for appreciation over time. As the real estate tycoon Barbara Corcoran famously said, "Don't wait to buy real estate. Buy real estate and wait." By leveraging the power of real estate, you can create a reliable income stream and build long-term wealth.

In addition to dividend stocks and real estate, there are various other income-generating assets that can contribute to your passive income arsenal. These include bonds, peer-to-peer lending, royalties from intellectual property, and even online businesses. The key is to diversify your income sources and explore opportunities that align with your risk tolerance and financial goals. Each income-generating asset has its own unique characteristics, and by carefully selecting and managing your portfolio, you can create a well-rounded mix of passive income streams.

Now, let's delve into the art of automating your income streams to minimize effort. The lazy millionaire understands the importance of creating systems and leveraging technology to maximize efficiency. One way to automate your passive income streams is through the use of digital platforms and online tools. For example, you can use robo-advisors to automate your investments in dividend stocks and other income-generating assets. These platforms use algorithms to manage your portfolio, rebalance it periodically, and reinvest dividends automatically. This eliminates the need for constant monitoring and decision-making, allowing you to enjoy the fruits of passive income with minimal effort.

Furthermore, technology has revolutionized the world of online businesses, offering opportunities to generate passive income through e-commerce, affiliate marketing, digital products, and more. By setting up online systems, automating processes, and leveraging digital marketing strategies, you can create a source of income that operates on autopilot. As the renowned entrepreneur Tim Ferriss once said, "Focus on being productive instead of busy." Automating your income streams frees up your time and energy to focus on other aspects of your lazy millionaire journey, such as decision-making and strategic planning.

In conclusion, passive income is the secret weapon of lazy millionaires—a powerful tool that allows us to generate income while minimizing effort. By diversifying our income sources through dividend stocks, real estate, and other income-generating assets, we create a resilient and consistent stream of passive income. Furthermore, by automating our income streams, we optimize efficiency and free up our time for more important endeavors. As we continue on our journey to lazy millionaire status, let us heed the wisdom of financial gurus and successful investors. Embrace the power of passive income, and unlock the extraordinary potential it holds in shaping your financial future.

In the next chapter, we will explore the art of strategic outsourcing—an essential skill for any aspiring lazy millionaire. By delegating tasks to experts and leveraging the power of outsourcing, we can further minimize our workload and focus on decision-making and strategic planning. Get ready to discover the art of building a team, creating a support system, and transforming yourself into a master of delegation. Until then, my fellow lazy millionaires-in-the-making, dream big, automate your income streams, and revel in the joy of financial freedom. The lazy millionaire lifestyle awaits you!

CHAPTER 5: THE ART OF OUTSOURCING: STREAMLINING YOUR SUCCESS

Welcome back, fellow lazy millionaires, to the exhilarating world of outsourcing—where the power of delegation and the art of streamlining converge to propel us towards effortless success. In this chapter, we will delve into the intricacies of identifying tasks that can be delegated or outsourced, finding the right freelancers, virtual assistants, and service providers, and streamlining our workflow by leveraging the expertise of others. So, fasten your seat belts and prepare to embark on a journey of streamlined efficiency and boundless productivity.

The first step in mastering the art of outsourcing is identifying the tasks that can be delegated or outsourced. Take a moment to reflect on your daily, weekly, and monthly responsibilities. Ask yourself, "Are there tasks that consume my time but do not require my specific expertise or attention?" These are the tasks that are prime candidates for delegation. By offloading these tasks, you create space for focusing on high-value activities that drive your success as a lazy millionaire.

Imagine this scenario: you're a budding entrepreneur with a brilliant business idea, and your time is precious. You possess a unique skill set and valuable insights that are vital to the growth of your business. However, mundane administrative tasks, such as managing emails, organizing files, or scheduling appointments, eat away at your productive hours. Instead of investing your precious time in these low-value activities, you can delegate them to a virtual assistant or administrative professional who specializes in these tasks. This frees up your time to focus on strategy, innovation, and decision-making—the activities that truly move the needle.

Once you've identified the tasks to delegate, the next step is finding the right freelancers, virtual assistants, and service providers who can seamlessly integrate into your operations. The digital landscape offers a vast array of platforms and resources to connect you with talented professionals from around the globe. Websites like Upwork, Freelancer, and Guru are treasure troves of skilled freelancers in various domains—ranging from graphic design and content writing to programming and marketing. These platforms provide you with the opportunity to review profiles, portfolios, and client feedback to ensure a good fit for your specific needs.

To find the perfect match, it's essential to clearly define the skills, qualifications, and experience you seek in a freelancer or service provider. Whether it's graphic design, website development, social media management, or customer support, outline your requirements with precision. Be open to exploring diverse talents and perspectives that can add value to your business. Remember, the key to successful outsourcing is not just finding someone to complete a task; it's about finding the right fit—a professional who shares your vision, understands your business, and delivers results in line with your expectations.

Consider this real-life example: Alex, an aspiring lazy millionaire, had a brilliant idea for an online store but lacked the technical expertise to build a website from scratch. Instead of investing time and energy into learning web development, Alex outsourced the task to a skilled web designer. The designer not only created a visually stunning and user-friendly website but also ensured seamless integration of e-commerce functionalities. By leveraging the expertise of a professional, Alex was able to launch the online store quickly and focus on other revenue-generating activities.

Streamlining your workflow is a critical component of the art of outsourcing. Once you have delegated tasks to freelancers or virtual assistants, it's essential to establish effective systems and communication channels to ensure a smooth workflow. Clearly communicate your expectations, deadlines, and desired outcomes to the individuals you have outsourced to. Establish regular check-ins and feedback loops to track progress, provide guidance, and address any questions or concerns.

Leveraging other people's expertise is not just about delegating tasks; it's about tapping into a pool of talent and knowledge that can take your business to new heights. Seek input and insights from your outsourced professionals. They may offer fresh perspectives, innovative ideas, and industry-specific knowledge that you may not possess. Remember, collaboration fuels growth, and by valuing the expertise of others, you position yourself as a savvy entrepreneur who knows how to leverage the collective genius of a team.

Let's take inspiration from Elon Musk, the visionary entrepreneur behind SpaceX and Tesla. Musk is known for his ability to delegate and trust in the expertise of his team members. He once said, "I think it is very important to have a feedback loop, where you're constantly thinking about what you've done and how you could be doing it better." By entrusting others with tasks that fall outside his core competencies, Musk maximizes his time and energy to focus on strategic decision-making and visionary thinking—the true drivers of his success.

In conclusion, the art of outsourcing is a game-changer for lazy millionaires. It enables us to delegate tasks that consume our time but don't require our expertise, find talented professionals who can seamlessly integrate into our operations, and streamline our workflow to achieve optimum efficiency. Remember to identify tasks that can be delegated, seek the right freelancers or service providers, and establish effective communication channels. Embrace collaboration and leverage the expertise of others to accelerate your journey to lazy millionaire greatness. Onward, fellow lazy millionaires, to streamlined success!

CHAPTER 6: BUILDING A DREAM TEAM

Welcome, fellow lazy millionaires, to the chapter that will revolutionize the way you approach your wealth-building journey —building a dream team. In this chapter, we will explore the importance of assembling a team of professionals who can handle different aspects of your financial endeavors. We'll discuss the roles of financial advisors, lawyers, accountants, and mentors, and how you can leverage their expertise to make informed decisions. So, get ready to witness the power of collaboration and surround yourself with a team that will propel you towards lazy millionaire greatness.

As you embark on your quest for financial freedom with minimal effort, it's crucial to acknowledge that you can't do it all alone. Building a dream team allows you to tap into the specialized knowledge and expertise of professionals who can guide and support you along the way. Let's delve into the key members of your dream team and the invaluable contributions they can make to your wealth-building journey.

The first member of your dream team is a financial advisor. A skilled financial advisor will help you navigate the complex world of investments, develop a tailored financial plan, and provide insights on wealth preservation and growth. They will analyze your financial goals, risk tolerance, and time horizon, and recommend investment strategies that align with your objectives. Remember, a lazy millionaire is not someone who takes unnecessary risks but rather someone who strategically allocates their resources for maximum returns.

Next up is a lawyer—an indispensable member of your team who will safeguard your interests and protect your assets. A knowledgeable lawyer will guide you through legal processes, draft contracts, and provide advice on estate planning, asset protection, and tax optimization. Their expertise will ensure that your financial endeavors comply with legal regulations and minimize potential risks. As the famous American jurist Oliver Wendell Holmes Jr. once said, "Lawyers spend a great deal of their time shoveling smoke."

Another crucial member of your dream team is an accountant. An experienced accountant will handle the intricacies of your financial records, tax filings, and financial reporting. They will help you optimize your tax strategies, identify cost-saving opportunities, and ensure compliance with financial regulations. By outsourcing your accounting tasks, you can focus on making strategic decisions and leave the number-crunching to the experts. As the brilliant entrepreneur Andrew Carnegie once stated, "The first man gets the oyster, the second man gets the shell."

Mentors are the secret sauce of any successful journey. Seek out individuals who have achieved the kind of financial success you aspire to and who embody the lazy millionaire mindset. A mentor can provide valuable guidance, share their experiences, and offer insights that can accelerate your progress. They can help you avoid common pitfalls, provide accountability, and inspire you to reach new heights. As the legendary entrepreneur and author Jim Rohn once said, "You are the average of the five people you spend the most time with." Surround yourself with mentors who push you to grow and challenge your limiting beliefs.

Remember, building a dream team is not just about hiring professionals—it's about nurturing relationships and fostering collaboration. Regularly communicate with your team members, share updates on your financial goals, and seek their input on important decisions. Collaboration allows you to leverage their expertise and gain multiple perspectives, leading to well-informed and balanced choices. As the iconic scientist Isaac Newton famously said, "If I have seen further, it is by standing on the shoulders of giants."

In conclusion, building a dream team is a crucial step on your lazy millionaire journey. These professionals—financial advisors, lawyers, accountants, and mentors—bring a wealth of knowledge and expertise to the table. They will guide and support you, helping you make informed decisions and navigate the complex world of finance. Remember, a team is only as strong as its weakest link, so choose your dream team members wisely. Together, you will conquer the challenges, seize the opportunities, and achieve the financial freedom you desire. Onward, lazy millionaires, to building your dream team and unlocking the next level of success!

CHAPTER 7: PASSIVE BUSINESS VENTURES: THE ART OF EFFORTLESS PROFIT

Welcome, my fellow lazy millionaires, to the exhilarating world of passive business ventures—where minimal effort meets maximum returns. In this chapter, we will dive deep into the realm of business ideas that offer passive income, explore the possibilities of licensing intellectual property, franchising, or investing in existing businesses, and discover the secrets of automating business operations to reduce our involvement. So, fasten your seat belts and prepare to embark on a journey of effortless profit and boundless freedom.

Passive income is the holy grail of lazy millionaires. It is income that flows into your bank account with little to no effort on your part. Imagine waking up each morning to a steady stream of income while sipping your favorite beverage, knowing that your business is generating revenue even when you're lounging on a tropical beach or pursuing your hobbies. That's the power of passive business ventures.

Let's explore some business ideas that can provide you with passive income. One option is licensing intellectual property. If you possess valuable intellectual property, such as patents, trademarks, or copyrighted works, you can license them to other businesses or individuals in exchange for royalties or licensing fees. This allows you to monetize your intellectual assets without actively engaging in day-to-day operations. Consider the success story of the legendary physicist Albert Einstein, whose theories and discoveries continue to generate passive income through licensing agreements and royalties.

Franchising is another lucrative avenue for lazy millionaires. By investing in a proven franchise system, you can benefit from an established brand, operational support, and a ready-made business model. Franchises allow you to leverage the success and reputation of existing businesses while minimizing your involvement. As the saying goes, "Why reinvent the wheel when you can buy the franchise?" Take inspiration from the fast-food giant McDonald's, which has built a global empire by offering franchise opportunities to aspiring entrepreneurs.

Investing in existing businesses is yet another pathway to passive income. Seek out businesses that have a track record of profitability, a strong management team, and a proven business model. By becoming a passive investor, you can reap the rewards of their success while minimizing your involvement in day-to-day operations. Warren Buffett, the legendary investor and billionaire, has achieved remarkable success by strategically investing in a diverse range of businesses and letting them grow under capable management teams.

Automation is the secret ingredient to passive business ventures. By leveraging technology and streamlining processes, you can minimize your direct involvement and create systems that generate income on autopilot. Implementing automation tools and software can help streamline operations, such as customer relationship management, order processing, inventory management, and marketing. This allows you to focus on the big picture and strategic decision-making while your business runs smoothly in the background. Think of automation as your silent butler, tirelessly working behind the scenes to ensure effortless profitability.

Let's take a fictional example to illustrate the power of passive business ventures. Meet Lily, a creative entrepreneur with a knack for designing unique home decor products. Instead of operating a traditional brick-and-mortar store, Lily decides to set up an online store where she can showcase and sell her creations. To minimize her involvement, Lily utilizes automation tools to handle inventory management, order processing, and shipping logistics. She also licenses her designs to other manufacturers who pay her royalties for each product sold. By leveraging technology, automation, and licensing, Lily creates a passive business venture that generates income while she focuses on designing new products and enjoying the fruits of her creativity.

In conclusion, passive business ventures hold the key to lazy millionaire success. Explore business ideas that offer passive income, such as licensing intellectual property, franchising, or investing in existing businesses. Embrace automation to streamline your operations and reduce your involvement. Remember, the goal is to create a business that works for you, not the other way around. With passive income flowing effortlessly into your bank account, you'll have more time to pursue your passions, enjoy the finer things in life, and savor the sweet taste of lazy millionaire success. Onward, fellow lazy millionaires, to effortless profit and endless freedom!

CHAPTER 8: THE POWER OF SYSTEMS AND AUTOMATION: UNLEASHING THE LAZY MILLIONAIRE'S ADVANTAGE

Ah, the sweet symphony of efficiency and automation—the secret ingredients behind the success of lazy millionaires worldwide. In this chapter, we will uncover the transformative power of implementing efficient systems and processes, harnessing the latest technology and software to streamline operations, and maximizing productivity while minimizing effort through the magic of automation. So, fasten your seat belts, my fellow lazy millionaires, as we embark on a journey to unlock the full potential of systems and automation.

Imagine a world where repetitive tasks vanish into thin air, where time-consuming processes become streamlined, and where your business hums along seamlessly without constant intervention. This is the world of systems and automation—a world where your focus shifts from mundane tasks to strategic decision-making and creative pursuits. The key lies in implementing efficient systems and processes that liberate your time and energy, allowing you to focus on what truly matters.

Efficiency is the heartbeat of every successful lazy millionaire. It's about finding the most effective and streamlined way to accomplish tasks, saving time and effort. By analyzing your workflow and identifying repetitive tasks, you can develop systems that automate these processes. This not only saves you valuable time but also minimizes the potential for errors or oversights that can derail your progress.

Let's dive into the world of systems and explore how they can revolutionize your business. Start by examining your daily operations and identifying tasks that consume a significant amount of your time. These tasks may include managing emails, organizing files, processing invoices, or even social media management. With the power of systems, you can automate these processes, freeing up your time for more important activities.

The first step in implementing efficient systems is to document your processes. Create clear, step-by-step instructions for each task, outlining the key actions, tools, and resources required. This documentation serves as a blueprint for automation, ensuring consistency and clarity as you build your automated workflows.

Now, let's explore the vast world of technology and software that can catapult your business into the realm of automation. From project management tools to customer relationship management (CRM) software, there's a plethora of options available to streamline your operations. Invest time in researching and selecting the right tools that align with your business needs. Remember, technology is your ally in the pursuit of laziness —it empowers you to automate tasks, manage data, and stay organized with minimal effort.

One example of automation in action is the use of chatbots. These virtual assistants can handle customer inquiries, provide support, and even process orders. By implementing a chatbot on your website or social media platforms, you can provide instant responses to customer queries without the need for manual intervention. This not only enhances the customer experience but also frees up your time to focus on strategic initiatives.

Another powerful tool in the lazy millionaire's arsenal is email automation. Instead of spending hours crafting individual emails or newsletters, you can utilize email automation software to schedule and send personalized messages to your audience. With just a few clicks, you can nurture leads, send follow-up emails, or deliver targeted content—all while you sip your favorite beverage and enjoy the leisurely life of a lazy millionaire.

Automation doesn't stop at communication and customer interactions. It extends to various aspects of your business, including inventory management, order processing, and data analysis. Consider implementing inventory management software that tracks stock levels, automatically places orders for replenishment, and generates real-time reports on inventory performance. By automating these processes, you can minimize manual errors, reduce inventory holding costs, and ensure timely order fulfillment.

As the saying goes, "Work smarter, not harder." Automation allows you to do just that by maximizing productivity and minimizing effort. By streamlining your operations and leveraging technology, you can achieve more in less time, giving you the freedom to focus on strategic decision-making and growth.

Take inspiration from the iconic businessman and investor, Richard Branson, who once said, "Automation is a gift to lazy people." Branson's Virgin Group has leveraged automation to streamline operations across its various ventures, allowing Branson to allocate his time and energy where it matters most —exploring new business opportunities and enjoying life to the fullest.

In conclusion, the power of systems and automation is the

lazy millionaire's advantage. By implementing efficient systems, documenting processes, and harnessing the latest technology and software, you can streamline your operations, maximize productivity, and minimize effort. Embrace the wonders of automation, and watch your business thrive while you enjoy the freedom that comes with being a lazy millionaire. Onward, my fellow lazy millionaires, to a world where systems and automation propel us to new heights of success!

CHAPTER 9: INVESTING IN YOURSELF: THE PATHWAY TO LAZY MILLIONAIRE GREATNESS

Welcome, dear lazy millionaires, to the exhilarating world of self-investment and personal growth—the magical realm where dreams are realized and fortunes are made. In this chapter, we shall delve deep into the importance of prioritizing self-improvement, investing in education, training, and acquiring new skills, and leveraging your knowledge and expertise to create a life of abundant leisure. So, strap on your learning cap, grab a cup of ambition (or perhaps a more leisurely beverage), and let's embark on a journey of self-discovery and financial success that would make even the laziest of millionaires proud.

A. Prioritizing self-improvement and personal growth: Because laziness should never be an excuse for stagnation.

Picture this: You, lounging on a plush recliner, with a book in one hand and a margarita in the other. Now, imagine that book is not just any book, but a treasure trove of wisdom and inspiration.

By prioritizing self-improvement, you can transform those lazy moments into powerful catalysts for personal growth.

Investing in yourself is like hitting the jackpot in the lazy millionaire's casino of life. It's about nourishing your mind, body, and soul, and becoming the best version of yourself. As the legendary entrepreneur Jim Rohn once proclaimed, "The only way it gets better for you is when you get better."

But fear not, fellow lazy millionaires, for self-improvement doesn't mean exhausting yourself with tedious tasks or long hours of hard work. It's about making small, meaningful changes that accumulate into a lifetime of growth and success.

So, how do you prioritize self-improvement without breaking a sweat? Start by setting aside dedicated time each day for personal development. Whether it's reading books, listening to educational podcasts, or engaging in activities that ignite your passions, these moments of intentional self-investment will pay dividends in the long run.

Consider the words of the great philosopher and mathematician, Bertrand Russell, who once said, "The good life is one inspired by love and guided by knowledge." So, let love be your motivation and knowledge be your guide as you embark on this lazy millionaire's journey of self-improvement.

B. Investing in education, training, and acquiring new skills: Because a lazy millionaire is a knowledgeable millionaire.

Ah, the joy of learning—the cornerstone of lazy millionaire greatness. Education is not limited to the hallowed halls of academia; it extends far beyond, encompassing a lifelong commitment to expanding your knowledge and acquiring new skills.

Investing in education is like adding fuel to the fire of your lazy millionaire ambitions. It's about embracing curiosity, seizing opportunities for growth, and unleashing the power of your mind. As the wise and witty Oscar Wilde once said, "You can never be overdressed or overeducated."

But fret not, dear lazy millionaires, for this is not a call to don the proverbial graduation cap and robe. Education comes in various forms, and the lazy millionaire knows how to make learning a delightful and effortless endeavor.

Explore online courses and certifications that align with your interests and goals. Whether it's mastering the art of stock trading or honing your marketing skills, there's a wealth of educational resources at your fingertips. Take advantage of the vast online universe and curate a personalized curriculum that caters to your lazy millionaire aspirations.

However, let us not forget the invaluable lessons that can be learned outside the confines of formal education. The late Steve Jobs, the visionary co-founder of Apple Inc., once remarked, "Stay hungry, stay foolish." Embrace the spirit of curiosity, embark on new adventures, and seek wisdom in unexpected places. For it is in the pursuit of unconventional knowledge that lazy millionaires often stumble upon the most extraordinary opportunities.

C. Leveraging your knowledge and expertise to create wealth: Because knowledge is not power until it's transformed into moolah.

Ah, the sweet symphony of knowledge and wealth intertwining. As a lazy millionaire, your journey of self-investment and education leads you to the golden gates of financial prosperity. But how do you unlock the vault and turn your knowledge and expertise into cold, hard cash?

It's time to unleash your inner entrepreneurial genius and explore the myriad ways to monetize your wisdom. Consider the story of Marie Forleo, the renowned entrepreneur and author, who famously said, "Clarity comes from engagement, not thought." By actively engaging with your knowledge and expertise, you can unlock the doors to lazy millionaire success.

One avenue for leveraging your knowledge is through consulting. As a lazy millionaire guru in your chosen field, you possess unique insights and expertise that others are willing to pay for. Offer your wisdom as a consultant, guiding individuals and businesses towards success while enjoying the freedom to work on your own terms.

Another avenue is public speaking. Take center stage, grab the microphone (preferably one with a golden handle), and share your knowledge with eager audiences. Inspire, educate, and entertain as you captivate the masses with your lazy millionaire wisdom. And remember, a standing ovation is the lazy millionaire's equivalent of a standing desk—optional.

Furthermore, consider the power of writing. Put pen to paper (or fingers to keyboard) and share your knowledge through books, blogs, or online publications. The written word has the remarkable ability to transcend time and space, reaching audiences far and wide. As the famous novelist Margaret Atwood once wrote, "A word after a word after a word is power."

Lastly, let us not forget the beauty of collaborations and partnerships. Surround yourself with like-minded individuals who complement your expertise and share your lazy millionaire vision. By pooling your collective knowledge and resources, you can embark on ambitious ventures and create wealth effortlessly.

In conclusion, investing in yourself is the key to lazy millionaire greatness. Prioritize self-improvement, indulge in the pleasures of education, and leverage your knowledge and expertise to unlock a life of abundance and leisure. Remember the words of Benjamin Franklin, one of history's wisest men, who said, "An investment in knowledge pays the best interest." So, my fellow lazy millionaires, let us embark on this transformative journey, where knowledge is our currency, and success is our reward. Onward to lazy millionaire enlightenment!

CHAPTER 10: MASTERING DECISION-MAKING: THE ART OF MAKING BIG BUCKS WITH MINIMAL BRAIN CELLS

Welcome, fellow lazy millionaires, to the captivating world of decision-making, where fortune favors the swift and the savvy. In this chapter, we shall unravel the secrets of developing effective decision-making strategies, identifying key decisions that have the most impact on your wealth, and learning to make informed choices quickly and efficiently. So, put on your thinking caps (or better yet, a stylish hat that screams "I'm making decisions in style"), and let's dive into the wild and wonderful realm of decision-making, lazy millionaire style.

A. Developing effective decision-making strategies: Because making decisions should be as effortless as sipping a piña colada on a tropical beach.

Picture this: You, reclining on a hammock, with a coconut drink in hand, pondering life's important decisions with the ease of a sloth on a Sunday afternoon. That, my dear lazy millionaires, is the epitome of effective decision-making.

To master the art of decision-making, one must first understand the power of intuition. As the wise and wacky Albert Einstein once quipped, "The intuitive mind is a sacred gift, and the rational mind is a faithful servant." Embrace your inner intuition and let it guide you through the treacherous waters of decision-making. After all, sometimes the heart knows what the spreadsheets don't.

However, don't let intuition be your only guiding light. Combine it with a dash of logical reasoning and a sprinkle of data analysis. Remember the words of the legendary investor Warren Buffett, who said, "In the business world, the rearview mirror is always clearer than the windshield." Take a peek at historical data, assess potential risks and rewards, and use your lazy millionaire wit to make calculated decisions.

Another powerful strategy is the art of delegation. Surround yourself with a team of experts and trusted advisors who can offer valuable insights and perspectives. As the great basketball coach Phil Jackson once remarked, "The strength of the team is each individual member. The strength of each member is the team." Together, you and your dream team can conquer the world of decision-making, one lazy choice at a time.

B. Identifying key decisions that have the most impact on your wealth: Because why make a hundred decisions when one can do the trick?

Dear lazy millionaires, let us not get lost in the sea of decision fatigue. Instead, let us focus on the decisions that truly move the needle and bring us closer to our wealth-building goals. Identify the key decisions that have the most impact and prioritize them like a lazy millionaire on a mission.

Consider the words of the wise and witty Tony Robbins, the famed life coach and motivational speaker, who said, "It is in your moments of decision that your destiny is shaped." Think of your decisions as stepping stones on the path to lazy millionaire greatness. Each decision has the power to catapult you closer to financial freedom or keep you stuck in the doldrums of mediocrity.

So, how do you identify these game-changing decisions? Start by assessing the potential return on investment (ROI) for each choice. Focus on decisions that have the highest potential for long-term wealth accumulation and minimal effort. Whether it's choosing the right investment opportunity or making strategic business moves, select the decisions that make the most significant impact with the least amount of work.

But beware the illusion of analysis paralysis. The lazy millionaire's path is paved with swift decisions and nimble actions. As the renowned author and entrepreneur Mark Twain once said, "Twenty years from now, you will be more disappointed by the things you didn't do than by the ones you did do." Embrace the art of decisive laziness and seize opportunities with gusto.

C. Learning to make informed choices quickly and efficiently: Because why waste time on decisions when there are sunny beaches waiting?

In the world of lazy millionaires, time is a precious commodity. We cannot afford to waste it deliberating endlessly over choices that could be made swiftly and efficiently. So, how do we become masters of quick and informed decision-making?

First and foremost, gather the necessary information and conduct due diligence. But remember, there is a fine line between thorough research and drowning in a sea of information. As the innovative business tycoon Richard Branson once said, "Screw it, let's do it!" Embrace a balance between acquiring essential knowledge and taking action. Trust your instincts, make informed choices, and set sail towards lazy millionaire triumph.

Additionally, practice the art of mental decluttering. Clear your mind of unnecessary noise and distractions. Find your Zen-like state amidst the chaos of decision-making. As the famous martial artist and actor Bruce Lee once mused, "Empty your mind, be formless, shapeless, like water." Let your thoughts flow freely, and allow the most crucial decisions to rise to the surface effortlessly.

Lastly, remember the power of laughter in decision-making. Studies have shown that a good chuckle can enhance creativity and decision-making abilities. So, my fellow lazy millionaires, sprinkle a pinch of humor into your decision-making process. As the hilarious comedian and actor Will Ferrell once said, "Before you marry a person, you should first make them use a computer with slow Internet service to see who they really are." Find humor in the process, and let it fuel your decision-making prowess.

In conclusion, mastering the art of decision-making is a fundamental skill for lazy millionaires. Develop effective strategies that combine intuition and logic, identify key decisions with the most impact, and learn to make informed choices quickly and efficiently. Remember the words of the legendary entrepreneur Elon Musk, who said, "When something is important enough, you do it even if the odds are not in your favor." Embrace the power of decision-making, my fellow lazy millionaires, and let it propel you towards a life of wealth, leisure, and laughter. Onward to decisive laziness!

CHAPTER 11: THE ART OF NEGOTIATION: THE LAZY MILLIONAIRE'S GUIDE TO GETTING MORE WITH LESS EFFORT

Ah, negotiation—the dance of the dealmakers, the art of getting what you want without breaking a sweat. In this chapter, we shall explore the enchanting world of negotiation and discover how mastering this skill can maximize your returns while minimizing your effort. So, put on your finest negotiating hat (or if you prefer, negotiating flip-flops) and let's dive into the exciting realm of wheeling, dealing, and getting the upper hand in any situation.

A. Mastering the art of negotiation to maximize returns and minimize effort: Because why settle for less when you can have it all?

Negotiation is an essential skill in the lazy millionaire's toolkit. It's like a magic wand that can transform ordinary deals into extraordinary opportunities. To become a master negotiator, one must understand the delicate balance between assertiveness and charm, the art of compromise, and the power of persuasion.

Take a page from the book of the great Winston Churchill, who once said, "To jaw-jaw is always better than to war-war." Negotiation is the civilized way of resolving conflicts and striking mutually beneficial agreements. It's about finding common ground and leaving everyone involved feeling like winners (even if you win a little more).

Start by setting clear goals and objectives before entering any negotiation. Know what you want, but be flexible enough to explore creative solutions. As the ingenious inventor and businessman Thomas Edison once said, "Opportunity is missed by most people because it is dressed in overalls and looks like work." Embrace the opportunity to negotiate and let it lead you to lazy millionaire triumph.

B. Negotiating deals, contracts, and partnerships: Because everything is negotiable (yes, even that extra slice of pizza).

Negotiation is not just about haggling over prices in flea markets. It's a skill that can be applied to various aspects of the lazy millionaire's life, from business deals to personal relationships (yes, even convincing your significant other to watch your favorite TV show).

When it comes to negotiating deals, keep in mind the timeless wisdom of the great business magnate and philanthropist, Warren Buffett, who said, "Price is what you pay. Value is what you get." Focus on the value you can bring to the table and use it as leverage in your negotiations. Remember, the lazy millionaire's mantra is to get more for less.

Contracts, oh contracts! They can be as thick as a phone book and twice as intimidating. But fear not, for negotiation can be your trusted ally in navigating these treacherous waters. Be thorough in reviewing the terms and conditions, and don't hesitate to negotiate for more favorable terms. As the brilliant legal mind and former Supreme Court Justice Ruth Bader Ginsburg once remarked, "Fight for the things that you care about, but do it in a way that will lead others to join you." Fight for your rights, my fellow lazy millionaires, and do it with finesse.

Partnerships are like a delicate tango—finding the right rhythm, trust, and mutual benefit. When negotiating partnerships, focus on aligning interests and fostering win-win scenarios. The charismatic entrepreneur and founder of Virgin Group, Richard Branson, once shared his approach to partnerships, saying, "A business has to be involving; it has to be fun, and it has to exercise your creative instincts." Seek partnerships that align with your vision, add value to your lazy millionaire empire, and make business a joyous adventure.

C. Leveraging your network and relationships to gain favorable outcomes: Because sometimes it's not just what you know, but who you know (or who owes you a favor).

In the realm of lazy millionaires, relationships are not just social currency; they are negotiation ammunition. Your network of contacts can open doors, create opportunities, and provide invaluable insights. So, nurture those relationships like you would a garden of money trees.

As the brilliant inventor and scientist, Albert Einstein once said, "The only source of knowledge is experience." Seek wisdom from those who have walked the path before you. Learn from their successes, failures, and negotiation triumphs. Surround yourself with mentors and advisors who can guide you through the treacherous negotiation terrains.

Remember, negotiation is not about bulldozing your way to victory; it's about building bridges and fostering long-term relationships. As the charismatic business magnate and TV personality, Oprah Winfrey, once said, "Surround yourself with only people who are going to lift you higher." Surround yourself with allies, my fellow lazy millionaires, and let them elevate your negotiation game to new heights.

In conclusion, the art of negotiation is a formidable weapon in the lazy millionaire's arsenal. Master this skill to maximize your returns and minimize your effort. Embrace the power of negotiation to strike deals, navigate contracts, and build fruitful partnerships. And never underestimate the power of your network and relationships in achieving favorable outcomes. As the famous playwright and poet, William Shakespeare, once wrote, "All the world's a stage, and all the men and women merely players." So, my fellow lazy millionaires, let us step onto the stage of negotiation, put on a grand performance, and secure the rewards we deserve. Onward to negotiating laziness!

CHAPTER 12: CREATING MULTIPLE STREAMS OF INCOME: BECAUSE ONE FLOW OF MONEY IS NEVER ENOUGH!

Welcome, dear lazy millionaires, to the chapter that will open the floodgates of financial abundance and turn your income into a magnificent symphony of cash flows. In this chapter, we shall delve into the art of creating multiple streams of income —a surefire way to increase your stability, fuel your wealth creation journey, and ensure that money comes to you from more directions than you can count (well, maybe not literally, but you get the idea).

A. Diversifying your income sources for increased stability and wealth creation: Because putting all your golden eggs in one basket is for amateurs.

Imagine this scenario: you have a single source of income—a job that pays the bills and keeps you afloat. But what if that source disappears? What if it dries up like a forgotten oasis in the desert? Well, my lazy millionaire friend, that's where diversification comes in.

Diversifying your income sources is like having an army of financial soldiers working for you, each with their own paycheck. It's about spreading your financial wings and exploring different avenues of wealth creation. As the famous investor and business magnate, Warren Buffett, once wisely stated, "Never depend on a single income. Make investment to create a second source."

So, how do you diversify? Well, you can start by exploring different industries or sectors. Look for opportunities where you can use your existing skills or knowledge to generate additional income. It could be starting a side business, investing in rental properties, or even exploring the world of online entrepreneurship. The options are as vast as the ocean (and just as potentially lucrative).

B. Exploring different business ventures and investment opportunities: Because lazy millionaires have a knack for finding the golden geese that lay the most lucrative eggs.

Let's face it—business ventures and investments are the playgrounds of the wealthy. But fear not, my lazy millionaire comrades, for you too can dabble in these exciting arenas without breaking a sweat (well, maybe just a little).

Consider the wise words of the renowned business tycoon and Shark Tank investor, Mark Cuban, who said, "The best investment you can make is in yourself." Start by investing in your own business ideas or ventures that align with your passions and skills. Remember, a successful business can generate a continuous stream of income while allowing you to maintain your lazy lifestyle.

But what if the thought of running a business sends shivers down your spine? Fear not! There are other investment opportunities waiting to be explored. From stocks and bonds to real estate and peer-to-peer lending, the investment world is like a buffet of financial possibilities. As the legendary investor and philanthropist, George Soros, once quipped, "The key to making money in stocks is not to get scared out of them." So, don't let fear hold you back from dipping your toes into the vast pool of investment opportunities.

C. Balancing risk and reward in your portfolio: Because even lazy millionaires know that fortune favors the cautious (and the hilarious).

Now, my dear lazy millionaires, let's talk about balance—no, not the kind you try to achieve on a yoga mat, but the delicate balance between risk and reward in your financial endeavors.

It's important to remember that with great reward comes some degree of risk (cue dramatic music). But fear not, my fellow risk-averse enthusiasts, for you can still navigate these treacherous waters with wit and humor (and maybe a life jacket or two, just in case).

Diversify your investment portfolio by allocating your funds across different asset classes. This will help spread the risk and minimize the impact of any single investment going awry. As the brilliant investor and co-founder of Berkshire Hathaway, Charlie Munger, once remarked, "The big money is not in the buying or the selling, but in the waiting."

Additionally, always keep an eye out for opportunities where the risk-reward ratio is tilted in your favor. Look for investments or ventures that have the potential for significant returns while minimizing the effort required on your part. Remember, my lazy millionaire amigos, it's about working smart, not hard.

In conclusion, creating multiple streams of income is like conducting a symphony of wealth. Diversify your income sources to increase stability and protect against unexpected financial downturns. Explore different business ventures and investment opportunities that align with your passions and skills. And most importantly, balance risk and reward in your portfolio to navigate the financial landscape with ease and humor. As the wise American industrialist, Henry Ford, once said, "Whether you think you can or think you can't, you're right." So, my fellow lazy millionaires, think big, think lazy, and let the multiple streams of income flow abundantly into your life.

CHAPTER 13: DEVELOPING PASSIVE INCOME ASSETS: UNLEASHING YOUR INNER CREATIVE GENIUS FOR MAXIMUM LAZINESS AND WEALTH!

Welcome, fellow lazy millionaires, to the chapter where we tap into the realms of creativity and innovation to develop passive income assets that will make money rain on us while we sip margaritas on a tropical beach (or wherever your lazy heart desires). Get ready to embrace your inner creative genius and let the wealth flow effortlessly into your bank account.

A. Creating and monetizing digital products or intellectual property: Because your brain is a treasure trove of lazy gold waiting to be exploited.

Ah, the wonders of the digital age! Never before has it been easier to turn your creative ideas and intellectual property into cold, hard cash. Whether you're a wordsmith, an artist, a musician, or a mastermind of unique concepts, there are endless opportunities to create and monetize digital products.

Consider the case of J.K. Rowling, the brilliant mind behind the Harry Potter series. From a simple idea born on a train journey, she created a magical world that captivated millions of readers worldwide. Her books, movies, merchandise, and even a theme park generate passive income to this day. So, unleash your creativity, my lazy millionaires, and explore the realms of e-books, online courses, digital art, music, or any other form of digital product that aligns with your talents and interests.

B. Generating royalties, licensing fees, and residual income: Because lazy millionaires know that making money while you sleep is the ultimate power move.

Imagine this—your creation, be it a book, a song, a patent, or a software, becomes a money-making machine that continues to churn out royalties and licensing fees long after you've put in the initial effort. Sounds like a dream, right? Well, my dear lazy millionaires, dreams do come true in the world of residual income.

Take the legendary musician and songwriter, Paul McCartney, for instance. His contributions to the Beatles' iconic catalog continue to generate royalties, securing him a steady stream of income without lifting a finger (or strumming a guitar string). So, find your creative niche, protect your intellectual property, and let the royalties roll in.

Licensing is another avenue to explore. By granting others the right to use your creation in exchange for a fee, you're essentially leveraging the power of your work to generate income without any additional effort on your part. It's like renting out a piece of your creative brilliance to others and letting them do the work while you reap the rewards. As the brilliant inventor and entrepreneur, Thomas Edison, once said, "To invent, you need a good imagination and a pile of junk." Well, my lazy millionaire friend, let your imagination soar and turn your creative genius into a lucrative licensing machine.

C. Building assets that continue to generate income with minimal effort: Because lazy millionaires love having their money work harder than they do.

Now, my fellow lazy millionaires, it's time to build assets that work tirelessly for you while you lounge in your favorite hammock, sipping on a refreshing beverage (umbrella optional).

Consider the wonders of real estate investing. By acquiring properties and renting them out, you're essentially building an army of income-generating soldiers that march to the beat of your laziness. As the real estate mogul and business magnate, Donald Trump, once said, "It's tangible, it's solid, it's beautiful. It's artistic, from my standpoint, and I just love real estate." So, let the properties do the heavy lifting while you enjoy the fruits of their labor.

But real estate is not the only option. From dividend-paying stocks and index funds to automated online businesses and vending machines, there's a myriad of assets that can generate passive income with minimal effort on your part. The key is to identify opportunities that align with your interests, risk tolerance, and desired level of involvement. Remember, my lazy millionaire comrade, it's all about finding the sweet spot where your assets work hard, so you don't have to.

In conclusion, developing passive income assets is like planting money trees that grow and flourish while you embrace your laziness. Create and monetize digital products or intellectual property, tap into the power of royalties and licensing fees, and build assets that continue to generate income with minimal effort. As the brilliant inventor and futurist, Nikola Tesla, once said, "The present is theirs; the future, for which I really worked, is mine." So, my lazy millionaire friend, let the future be yours as you embark on the journey of developing passive income assets and basking in the glory of effortless wealth.

CHAPTER 14: OUTSOURCING PERSONAL FINANCES: BECAUSE EVEN LAZY MILLIONAIRES NEED A FINANCIAL DREAM TEAM!

Welcome, my fellow lazy millionaires, to the chapter where we unleash the power of delegation and outsource the tedious task of personal finance management to the experts. Get ready to assemble your financial dream team and let them handle the nitty-gritty while you focus on the important things in life, like binge-watching your favorite TV show or perfecting your cocktail mixing skills.

A. Delegating personal finance management to professionals: Because let's face it, numbers and spreadsheets are not exactly our idea of a good time.

We all know that managing personal finances can be as exciting as watching paint dry or listening to a never-ending lecture on quantum physics. But fear not, my fellow lazy millionaires, for there are professionals out there who thrive on numbers, spreadsheets, and all things money-related.

Consider the story of Warren Buffett, the legendary investor and one of the richest people on the planet. Despite his immense wealth and financial prowess, Buffett has a team of financial advisors and analysts who assist him in managing his vast empire. Why? Because even the Oracle of Omaha knows that delegating certain tasks allows him to focus on what he does best —making brilliant investment decisions.

So, follow in the footsteps of Buffett and surround yourself with financial professionals who can handle the complexities of personal finance management. From accountants and bookkeepers to financial planners and wealth managers, let them take care of the budgeting, tax planning, investment strategies, and all the other mind-numbing tasks that come with managing your wealth. After all, why crunch numbers when you can let someone else do it while you sit back and enjoy the sweet taste of laziness?

B. Hiring financial planners and advisors to handle investments and wealth management: Because making money is their bread and butter, and you deserve a taste of that buttery goodness.

Investments can be like a maze, full of twists, turns, and hidden pitfalls. But worry not, my lazy millionaire friend, for there are financial planners and advisors who can navigate the labyrinth on your behalf.

Picture this: You're on a treasure hunt, and the treasure is maximum wealth with minimal effort. Your financial planner is the guide who holds the map and leads you through the twists and turns of the investment landscape. With their expertise, they can help you make informed decisions, manage risk, and optimize your portfolio for maximum returns.

Take the advice of the legendary investor, Peter Lynch, who

famously said, "Know what you own, and know why you own it." By hiring a financial advisor, you not only benefit from their knowledge and experience but also gain a deeper understanding of your investments and the reasons behind them. It's like having a personal financial Sherpa who ensures you reach the summit of wealth while you enjoy the scenic views.

So, my lazy millionaire companion, let the financial wizards crunch the numbers, analyze the markets, and handle the complexities of wealth management. It's their domain, and by outsourcing this aspect of your financial life, you free up your time and mental energy to focus on the things that truly matter to you.

C. Optimizing your financial strategies to minimize your involvement: Because life is too short to spend it buried in spreadsheets.

Let's face it, my lazy millionaire compadres, our time is precious, and we would rather spend it on the things we love, like sipping cocktails by the pool or embarking on spontaneous adventures. That's why optimizing our financial strategies to minimize our involvement is the smart way to go.

Consider the story of Richard Branson, the iconic entrepreneur and founder of the Virgin Group. Branson understands the value of efficiency and delegation, and he has built a global empire by focusing on what he does best while delegating the rest. By leveraging the expertise of others and optimizing his business and financial strategies, he has managed to achieve great success while enjoying a life of adventure and leisure.

Apply this same principle to your personal finances. Look for ways to streamline your financial processes, automate repetitive tasks, and leverage technology to simplify your life. From setting up automatic bill payments and online banking to using budgeting apps and investment platforms, embrace the wonders of modern technology that allow you to manage your finances with minimal effort.

Remember, my fellow lazy millionaires, you don't have to be a financial wizard to build and maintain wealth. By delegating personal finance management to professionals, hiring financial planners and advisors, and optimizing your financial strategies, you can achieve financial success while basking in the glory of laziness. As the great inventor and businessman, Thomas Edison, once said, "Opportunity is missed by most people because it is dressed in overalls and looks like work." So, let's leave the overalls to those who enjoy them and embrace the opportunities that come with being a lazy millionaire.

In conclusion, my fellow lazy millionaires, it's time to unleash the power of delegation and outsource the mundane task of personal finance management. By assembling a financial dream team, hiring professionals, and optimizing your strategies, you can achieve financial success while enjoying the sweet taste of laziness. So, raise your glass (preferably filled with a refreshing beverage) and toast to a life of effortless wealth!

CHAPTER 15: THE POWER OF NETWORKING: MAKING CONNECTIONS THE LAZY MILLIONAIRE WAY

Welcome, my fellow lazy millionaires, to the chapter where we unlock the secrets of networking without breaking a sweat. In this digital age, building a strong network is essential for success, and we're here to show you how to do it with minimal effort. So put on your most comfortable slippers, grab a cup of coffee, and get ready to expand your reach, influence, and opportunities without even leaving your cozy couch.

A. Building a strong network of like-minded individuals and experts: Because who needs boring business cards when you can connect with people who share your passion for laziness?

Networking doesn't have to be a tedious affair of exchanging business cards and engaging in small talk at dull conferences. Instead, let's focus on building genuine connections with like-minded individuals who understand and appreciate the lazy millionaire lifestyle.

Seek out communities, both online and offline, that align with your interests and values. Whether it's joining a mastermind group of successful entrepreneurs or becoming a member of a social club that caters to your hobbies, surround yourself with people who inspire and motivate you.

Take inspiration from the late Steve Jobs, the visionary co-founder of Apple, who famously said, "Your work is going to fill a large part of your life, and the only way to be truly satisfied is to do what you believe is great work. And the only way to do great work is to love what you do." By connecting with individuals who share your passions and beliefs, you create a supportive network that can propel you toward success.

So, my fellow lazy millionaires, put your networking skills to work by seeking out like-minded individuals who understand and appreciate your unique approach to wealth-building. Remember, it's not about the quantity of connections; it's about the quality and depth of those connections.

B. Leveraging connections for opportunities, partnerships, and collaborations: Because a lazy millionaire knows how to turn connections into golden opportunities.

Networking isn't just about collecting contacts in your virtual rolodex; it's about leveraging those connections to create exciting opportunities, partnerships, and collaborations. Think of it as building a web of lazy millionaire allies who can help you achieve your goals without breaking a sweat.

Take a page from the book of Elon Musk, the visionary entrepreneur behind Tesla and SpaceX. Musk is known for his ability to forge strategic partnerships that have propelled his companies to new heights. From partnering with NASA to revolutionize space exploration to collaborating with major automakers to accelerate the electric vehicle revolution, Musk knows the power of leveraging connections for success.

So, my lazy millionaire friend, don't hesitate to reach out to your network when opportunities arise. Whether it's a potential business partnership, a speaking engagement, or a collaboration on a passion project, let your connections be the springboard to your success. Remember, success is not a solo journey; it's a team effort.

C. Expanding your reach and influence with minimal effort: Because the lazy millionaire knows how to make a big impact without lifting a finger (well, maybe just one finger for a click).

In the digital age, expanding your reach and influence has never been easier, and the lazy millionaire knows how to capitalize on the power of technology to make a big impact. With just a few clicks, you can reach thousands, if not millions, of people around the world.

Embrace the wonders of social media and online platforms to amplify your message and extend your influence. Share your wisdom, insights, and witty observations through blog posts, videos, podcasts, or social media content. Engage with your audience, respond to comments, and build a loyal following of lazy millionaire enthusiasts who hang on to your every word (or at least click the like button).

Look at the example of Gary Vaynerchuk, the social media guru and entrepreneur who built his empire by leveraging the power of online platforms. Vaynerchuk used his unique blend of humor, authenticity, and valuable content to establish himself as a thought leader and build a massive online following.

So, my fellow lazy millionaires, use the digital tools at your disposal to extend your reach and influence. Don't be afraid to share your expertise, entertain your audience, and make a lasting impact. Remember, a lazy millionaire knows how to make a big splash with just a little effort.

In conclusion, my fellow lazy millionaires, networking doesn't have to be a chore. It can be an enjoyable and fruitful endeavor that aligns with your lazy lifestyle. By building a strong network of like-minded individuals, leveraging connections for opportunities and collaborations, and expanding your reach and influence with minimal effort, you can achieve great success while sipping your favorite beverage from the comfort of your recliner.

As the famous comedian and actor, Groucho Marx, once said, "I find television very educational. Every time someone turns it on, I go into another room and read a book." So, let's put our lazy millionaire spin on networking and make meaningful connections without leaving our cozy spaces. Cheers to lazy networking and a life of effortless connections!

CHAPTER 16: LEVERAGING TECHNOLOGY FOR FINANCIAL SUCCESS: EMBRACE THE GEEKY SIDE OF LAZY MILLIONAIRES

Welcome, my fellow lazy millionaires, to the exciting world of financial technology, where you can achieve financial success without lifting a finger (okay, maybe just a few taps on your smartphone). In this chapter, we will dive into the realm of technology and discover how it can revolutionize your financial journey. So put on your virtual reality goggles, grab your smart device, and get ready to embrace the geeky side of lazy millionaires!

A. Utilizing technology tools and platforms to automate financial tasks: Because why manually balance your checkbook when you can let technology do the heavy lifting?

Gone are the days of tedious financial tasks that drain your energy. With the help of technology, you can automate and streamline your financial management like a pro. Say goodbye to stacks of paperwork and hello to a world where technology takes care of the nitty-gritty details.

Imagine having a personal finance assistant who keeps track of your expenses, sends you reminders for bill payments, and even provides insights on how to optimize your budget. Well, that's the magic of financial management apps like Mint or Personal Capital. These smart tools utilize advanced algorithms and data analysis to simplify your financial life and help you make informed decisions.

As the late tech pioneer, Steve Jobs, once said, "Technology is nothing. What's important is that you have a faith in people, that they're basically good and smart, and if you give them tools, they'll do wonderful things with them." So, let's put our faith in technology and let it do the wonderful things it's designed to do— make our financial lives easier and more efficient.

B. Exploring fintech solutions, robo-advisors, and AI-powered financial services: Because who needs a traditional financial advisor when you can have a robot in a suit?

Gone are the days of stuffy boardrooms and traditional financial advisors. Now, you can embrace the era of fintech solutions and robo-advisors that offer smart and personalized financial advice at the touch of a button. It's like having a financial advisor in your pocket, minus the expensive fees and formal attire.

Take, for example, the rise of robo-advisors like Betterment or Wealthfront. These digital investment platforms utilize sophisticated algorithms and AI technology to create and manage investment portfolios tailored to your goals and risk tolerance. It's like having a team of financial experts at your disposal, working tirelessly to grow your wealth while you kick back and relax.

As the famous investor and philanthropist, Warren Buffett, once said, "Price is what you pay. Value is what you get." With fintech solutions and robo-advisors, you get exceptional value for your investment without the hefty price tag. So, let's embrace the robot revolution and let them handle the complex financial tasks while we focus on more important things, like binge-watching our favorite shows or perfecting our golf swing.

C. Maximizing your financial efficiency with the help of technology: Because a lazy millionaire knows how to make technology work for them, not the other way around.

Technology isn't just about automating tasks and getting personalized advice; it's also about maximizing your financial efficiency. With the right tools and platforms, you can make smarter financial decisions, optimize your investments, and keep a pulse on your financial health—all with minimal effort.

Let's take a moment to appreciate the power of online banking and mobile payment apps. They allow us to manage our finances, transfer funds, and even pay bills with a few taps on our smartphones. It's like having a personal banking concierge in the palm of your hand, making financial transactions a breeze.

And who can forget the wonders of online marketplaces and peer-to-peer lending platforms? They provide us with opportunities to diversify our investment portfolio, invest in real estate or startups, and earn passive income—all without leaving the comfort of our recliners. It's a lazy millionaire's dream come true!

As the legendary entrepreneur and founder of Virgin Group, Sir Richard Branson, once said, "I have enjoyed life a lot more by saying 'yes' than by saying 'no'." So, let's say 'yes' to the wonders of technology and explore the endless possibilities it offers for our financial success.

In conclusion, my fellow lazy millionaires, technology is your secret weapon on the path to financial success. By utilizing technology tools and platforms to automate financial tasks, exploring fintech solutions and robo-advisors for personalized advice, and maximizing your financial efficiency with the help of technology, you can achieve your financial goals with minimal effort.

Remember, technology is here to enhance our lives and make our lazy millionaire journey even more enjoyable. So, embrace your inner geek, tap into the power of technology, and let it propel you towards financial greatness while you sip your favorite beverage and enjoy the fruits of your laziness. Cheers to the geeky side of lazy millionaires!

CHAPTER 17: INVESTING IN REAL ESTATE WITH MINIMAL EFFORT: THE LAZY MILLIONAIRE'S GUIDE TO PROPERTY PROFITS

Welcome, my fellow lazy millionaires, to the glamorous world of real estate investing, where you can build your wealth without breaking a sweat. In this chapter, we will uncover the secrets of investing in real estate with minimal effort, because who needs to swing a hammer or deal with tenants when you can sit back and watch the cash flow in? So, put on your imaginary hard hat and let's dive into the world of effortless property profits!

A. Exploring real estate investment strategies that require little active involvement: Because who needs to get their hands dirty when you can let others do the heavy lifting?

When it comes to real estate investing, there are plenty of strategies that allow you to reap the rewards without getting your hands dirty. One such strategy is investing in turnkey properties.

These are fully renovated and managed properties that are ready to generate rental income from day one. It's like buying a delicious cake without having to bake it yourself—just sit back and enjoy the sweet taste of passive income.

As the real estate mogul and TV personality, Donald Trump, once said, "I made a lot of money in real estate, and I'll make a lot more in the future." So, let's take a page from his book and explore the world of turnkey properties, where you can make money while sipping your favorite cocktail on the beach.

B. Investing in REITs, or real estate crowdfunding: Because who needs to buy an entire building when you can own a piece of many?

If the idea of managing individual properties doesn't appeal to your lazy millionaire sensibilities, fear not! There are alternative options that allow you to invest in real estate without the hassle. One such option is investing in Real Estate Investment Trusts (REITs), which are companies that own and manage income-generating properties. By investing in REITs, you become a shareholder and can enjoy the benefits of real estate ownership without the headaches.

As the business magnate and philanthropist, Warren Buffett, once said, "Price is what you pay. Value is what you get." REITs provide an opportunity to tap into the value of real estate without the hefty price tag of buying properties outright. It's like enjoying a delicious slice of pizza without having to make the whole pie yourself.

Another exciting option is real estate crowdfunding, where you can pool your funds with other investors to invest in larger properties or real estate projects. It's like joining forces with a group of like-minded individuals to unlock the potential of real estate without taking on all the responsibilities.

C. Outsourcing property management and maintenance: Because

who needs to deal with leaky faucets and demanding tenants when you can have a team of professionals handle it for you?

If the idea of being a landlord makes you cringe, fret not, my fellow lazy millionaires. You can outsource the property management and maintenance tasks to professionals who will handle the day-to-day operations for you. It's like having a superhero team swoop in to save the day while you relax in your secret lair.

Imagine having a property management company that takes care of finding and screening tenants, collecting rent, and handling repairs and maintenance. It's like having your own personal army of real estate experts working tirelessly to keep your investment running smoothly.

As the real estate tycoon and business magnate, Sam Zell, once said, "Real estate is my life, but the people are more important than buildings." So, let's prioritize our own well-being and happiness by entrusting the management of our properties to professionals, allowing us to focus on the things that truly matter, like savoring a delicious meal or embarking on an adventure.

In conclusion, my fellow lazy millionaires, investing in real estate with minimal effort is not only possible but also highly lucrative. By exploring real estate investment strategies that require little active involvement, such as investing in turnkey properties or REITs, and by outsourcing property management and maintenance tasks to professionals, you can enjoy the benefits of real estate ownership without the sweat and tears.

Remember, as the legendary investor and philanthropist, John D. Rockefeller, once said, "The major fortunes in America have been made in land." So, let's seize the opportunity to build our own fortunes while reclining in our luxurious chairs, sipping our favorite beverages, and relishing the delights of the lazy millionaire lifestyle. Cheers to effortless property profits, my friends!

CHAPTER 18: OUTSOURCING MARKETING AND SALES: LET THE EXPERTS SELL YOUR WAY TO SUCCESS!

Welcome, my savvy entrepreneurs, to the exciting world of outsourcing marketing and sales. In this chapter, we will explore how you can harness the power of professionals and cutting-edge technology to boost your business without lifting a finger. So, sit back, relax, and get ready to watch your sales soar while sipping your favorite beverage. Cheers to effortless marketing and sales success!

A. Leveraging marketing agencies or freelancers to handle marketing efforts: Because why spend countless hours trying to navigate the treacherous waters of marketing when there are experts who can do it for you?

Marketing is like a wild jungle filled with elusive customers and ferocious competition. It requires strategy, creativity, and a knack for capturing attention. But fear not, my fellow entrepreneurs, for there are marketing agencies and talented freelancers who have mastered the art of taming this wild beast.

As the marketing guru Seth Godin once said, "Marketing is no longer about the stuff that you make, but about the stories you tell." By enlisting the help of marketing experts, you can unleash captivating stories about your brand and products, reaching your target audience with precision and finesse.

Imagine having a team of skilled professionals crafting compelling advertisements, engaging social media campaigns, and irresistible content on your behalf. It's like having an army of marketing superheroes working tirelessly to promote your business while you enjoy a well-deserved nap.

B. Automating sales processes and utilizing e-commerce platforms: Because who needs to manually handle transactions when technology can do it for you?

Sales can be a demanding and time-consuming task, but luckily, we live in the digital age where technology can be our loyal sales assistant. By automating sales processes and utilizing e-commerce platforms, you can streamline your operations and free up valuable time for more important matters, like perfecting your golf swing or binge-watching your favorite TV series.

As the innovative entrepreneur Elon Musk once said, "You want to be extra rigorous about making the best possible thing you can. Find everything that's wrong with it and fix it." Automation allows you to eliminate errors and create a seamless sales experience for your customers.

Imagine having an e-commerce platform that effortlessly handles product listings, order processing, and secure transactions. It's like having a virtual salesperson working around the clock, never asking for a raise or taking a coffee break.

C. Minimizing your involvement in marketing and sales activities: Because life is too short to be stuck in a never-ending sales pitch.

As an entrepreneur, your time is precious, and your talents should be utilized where they truly shine. By minimizing your involvement in marketing and sales activities, you can focus on what you do best, whether it's designing groundbreaking products or brainstorming innovative ideas.

As the business magnate and philanthropist Richard Branson once said, "The best way of learning about anything is by doing." So, let's apply this wisdom to our own businesses and delegate marketing and sales tasks to those who have honed their craft. It's like having a dream team of experts who will make your business shine while you kick back and enjoy the fruits of their labor.

Remember, my entrepreneurial friends, outsourcing marketing and sales is not a sign of weakness but a smart business move. By harnessing the expertise of professionals and leveraging technology, you can catapult your business to new heights while maintaining your sanity and zest for life.

In conclusion, outsourcing marketing and sales is the secret weapon that allows you to conquer the market with ease. By tapping into the talents of marketing agencies or freelancers, automating sales processes, and minimizing your involvement in marketing and sales activities, you can achieve unprecedented success without breaking a sweat.

So, raise your glass to the power of outsourcing, where you can focus on what you do best and let the experts handle the rest. Cheers to effortless marketing and sales domination, my fellow entrepreneurs!

CHAPTER 19: PASSIVE INCOME THROUGH INTELLECTUAL PROPERTY: UNLEASHING THE HIDDEN GOLDMINE OF CREATIVITY

Welcome, my creative comrades, to the enchanting realm of passive income through intellectual property. In this chapter, we will embark on a journey of unleashing your artistic genius and turning it into a steady stream of income that flows effortlessly into your pocket. So, grab your paintbrush, tune your guitar, or open your writing pad, because we're about to dive into the magical world of monetizing your creativity.

A. Creating and monetizing books, music, or artwork: Because your imagination knows no bounds, and your talent deserves to be celebrated and rewarded.

Imagine your words dancing across the pages of a bestselling book, captivating readers around the world with your storytelling prowess. Picture your melodies floating through the airwaves, touching the hearts of millions with their irresistible charm. Visualize your artwork adorning the walls of galleries, attracting art enthusiasts who are eager to possess a piece of your creative brilliance.

As the legendary author J.K. Rowling once said, "I do believe something very magical can happen when you read a good book." By creating and monetizing your books, music, or artwork, you have the power to create that magic and let it ripple through the lives of others.

B. Licensing intellectual property for royalties and residual income: Because your creations have the potential to unlock a lifetime of passive wealth.

Licensing your intellectual property is like opening the gates to a treasure trove of royalties and residual income. It's the art of turning your creations into assets that continue to generate income long after the initial creation is complete.

Imagine your book being adapted into a blockbuster movie, with each ticket sold adding to your ever-growing royalty checks. Envision your music being used in commercials, TV shows, and films, earning you a constant flow of licensing fees. Enthralling, isn't it?

As the musical genius Bob Dylan once sang, "The times, they are a-changin'." In today's digital age, opportunities for licensing intellectual property abound. From partnering with companies for merchandise featuring your artwork to licensing your music for video games and advertisements, the possibilities are limited only by your imagination.

C. Leveraging online platforms for exposure and passive income generation: Because the internet is a vast playground where your creations can thrive and make money while you sleep.

Thanks to the digital revolution, artists like you can showcase their talents to a global audience without leaving the comfort of their creative sanctuary. Online platforms have become the gateway to exposure and passive income generation.

Imagine uploading your artwork to an online gallery, where art enthusiasts from every corner of the world can discover and purchase your masterpieces. Envision self-publishing your books on platforms like Amazon Kindle, reaching readers across the globe and receiving a steady flow of royalties. How exciting!

As the tech entrepreneur and investor Naval Ravikant once said, "The Internet has massively broadened the possible space of careers. Most people haven't figured this out yet." By leveraging online platforms, you can tap into this vast potential and transform your creativity into a lucrative venture.

In conclusion, passive income through intellectual property is a pathway to financial freedom for the artists and creatives of the world. By creating and monetizing books, music, or artwork, licensing your intellectual property, and leveraging online platforms, you can turn your passion into a sustainable source of income that flows effortlessly into your bank account.

So, my creative comrades, embrace the power of your imagination, unleash your artistic brilliance, and let your creations pave the way to a life of abundance. The world is waiting to be enchanted by your talent, and your bank account is ready to be sprinkled with the magic of passive income.

Remember, creativity knows no bounds, and neither should your income. So, paint, write, compose, and create your way to financial prosperity. Your masterpieces await, and so does your destiny as a thriving artist in the realm of passive income.

CHAPTER 20: THE LAZY MILLIONAIRE'S INVESTMENT PORTFOLIO: EFFORTLESSLY BUILDING WEALTH WITH STYLE

Welcome, dear readers, to the world of the lazy millionaire—an oasis where financial abundance is attained with minimal effort and maximum returns. In this chapter, we will unveil the secrets of designing an investment portfolio that not only grows your wealth but does so while you sip on a piña colada by the pool. So, kick back, relax, and let's embark on this journey of lazy financial success.

A. Designing an investment portfolio tailored for minimal effort and maximum returns: Because why work harder when you can work smarter and let your money do the heavy lifting?

As the brilliant investor Warren Buffett once quipped, "Rule No. 1: Never lose money. Rule No. 2: Never forget Rule No. 1." By designing an investment portfolio that requires minimal effort, you not only mitigate the risks but also set yourself up for long-term success.

Imagine a portfolio that hums along smoothly without constant monitoring or active management. Visualize investments that steadily appreciate in value while you focus on more important things—like deciding which flavor of ice cream to indulge in.

B. Diversifying across different asset classes and investment vehicles: Because putting all your eggs in one basket is for amateurs, and lazy millionaires prefer a diversified brunch.

As the legendary investor Ray Dalio once said, "Diversification is a highly effective way to reduce risk." By spreading your investments across different asset classes and investment vehicles, you create a well-balanced buffet of financial opportunities.

Picture owning a mix of stocks, bonds, real estate, and even a sprinkle of alternative investments like fine wine or rare Pokémon cards. By diversifying, you ensure that the success of your portfolio isn't solely dependent on a single asset or industry.

C. Automating investment contributions and rebalancing: Because laziness and financial success go hand in hand when technology does the heavy lifting.

In today's era of cutting-edge technology, why manually manage your investments when you can automate the entire process? With a few clicks and a little bit of programming prowess, you can set up automatic contributions to your investment accounts and even automate the rebalancing of your portfolio.

Imagine waking up to find that your investment accounts have magically grown overnight—thanks to the wonders of automation. Envision the joy of knowing that your portfolio is consistently aligned with your risk tolerance and investment goals without lifting a finger.

As the tech visionary Elon Musk once quipped, "I would like to die on Mars. Just not on impact." Well, dear reader, with automated investments, you can aim for the stars without worrying about crash landings.

In conclusion, the lazy millionaire's investment portfolio is a testament to the fact that you can build wealth without breaking a sweat. By designing a portfolio tailored for minimal effort, diversifying across different asset classes, and automating contributions and rebalancing, you set yourself up for financial success while enjoying the finer things in life—like napping in a hammock or binge-watching your favorite TV show.

So, my fellow lazy millionaires, embrace the power of effortless wealth creation, where your money works harder than you do. Sit back, relax, and let your investment portfolio take you on a luxurious journey to financial independence. After all, life is too short to spend it toiling away when you can achieve greatness with a touch of laziness.

Remember, fortune favors the lazy—especially when it comes to building a million-dollar investment portfolio.

CHAPTER 21: MINDFUL WEALTH MANAGEMENT: BALANCING FINANCIAL SUCCESS AND PERSONAL BLISS

Welcome, dear readers, to the realm of mindful wealth management—a place where financial success and personal well-being dance harmoniously to the rhythm of abundance. In this chapter, we will delve into the art of balancing your bank account and your inner peace, all while maintaining a witty and humorous outlook on life. So, grab your yoga mat, find your center, and let's embark on this mindful journey to prosperity.

A. Adopting a mindful approach to wealth management: Because being present in the pursuit of wealth is far more satisfying than mindlessly chasing money like a squirrel after nuts.

As the wise Buddhist monk Thich Nhat Hanh once said, "Smile, breathe, and go slowly." Mindful wealth management begins with the awareness of your financial goals and the intention to align your actions with your aspirations.

Imagine consciously making financial decisions, aware of the impact they have on your life and the lives of others. Picture yourself investing in companies that align with your values and contribute positively to society. By being mindful, you can create a financial roadmap that brings both material wealth and a sense of purpose.

B. Balancing financial success with personal well-being and fulfillment: Because money can buy many things, but it can't buy happiness—unless you're purchasing ice cream, that is.

As the legendary investor and philanthropist, Warren Buffett once remarked, "Someone is sitting in the shade today because someone planted a tree a long time ago." Mindful wealth management recognizes that financial success is not an end in itself but a means to a fulfilling life.

Imagine pursuing your passions, nurturing your relationships, and taking care of your physical and mental well-being. By striking a balance between financial success and personal fulfillment, you can create a life of abundance that encompasses more than just money.

C. Cultivating a lifestyle that aligns with your values and priorities: Because being rich is not just about the size of your bank account, but about the richness of your experiences.

As the renowned author and motivational speaker, Jim Rohn, wisely observed, "You are the average of the five people you spend the most time with." Mindful wealth management encourages you to surround yourself with people who uplift and inspire you, fostering a supportive community that aligns with your values and aspirations.

Imagine living a life that reflects your priorities, whether it's spending quality time with loved ones, contributing to causes you believe in, or pursuing personal growth and self-care. By cultivating a lifestyle that aligns with your values, you can create a sense of fulfillment that money alone can never provide.

In conclusion, mindful wealth management is an invitation to infuse consciousness and intentionality into your financial journey. By adopting a mindful approach, balancing financial success with personal well-being, and cultivating a lifestyle that aligns with your values, you can achieve a state of abundance that encompasses both material wealth and inner fulfillment.

So, my fellow mindful wealth managers, let us embark on this journey of conscious prosperity—where financial success and personal bliss coexist in perfect harmony. Remember, life is too precious to be solely focused on numbers on a balance sheet. Embrace the joy of living, cherish your relationships, and seek fulfillment in every aspect of your journey toward abundance.

May your financial decisions be mindful, your bank account flourish, and your heart overflow with gratitude. Here's to a life of wealth in all its dimensions—the kind that enriches your soul and leaves a positive impact on the world around you.

CHAPTER 22: ESCAPING THE TIME-FOR-MONEY TRAP: A HILARIOUS JOURNEY TO TIME AND MONEY FREEDOM

Ah, the infamous time-for-money trap—a sticky spiderweb that catches us all in its clutches at some point in our lives. But fear not, dear reader, for in this chapter, we shall embark on a hilarious adventure to break free from this web and achieve the elusive time and money freedom we all desire. So put on your superhero cape, buckle up, and get ready to soar into a life of leisure and personal pursuits!

A. Breaking free from the traditional 9-to-5 job and trading time for money: Because life is too short to be chained to a desk from dawn till dusk like a caffeinated hamster on a wheel.

As the legendary comedian and actor Jim Carrey once quipped, "I think everybody should get rich and famous and do everything they ever dreamed of so they can see that it's not the answer." Breaking free from the time-for-money trap begins with a realization that there's more to life than punching a clock and waiting for weekends to arrive.

Picture yourself sipping margaritas on a beach while your passive income streams fill your bank account. Imagine having the freedom to pursue your passions, spend time with loved ones, and explore the world at your leisure. By thinking outside the cubicle and exploring alternative income sources, you can bid farewell to the monotonous 9-to-5 grind.

B. Creating passive income streams that allow for time and location freedom: Because who wouldn't want to make money while lounging in their pajamas or sipping coffee at a cozy café?

As the business magnate and investor, Warren Buffett, wisely stated, "If you don't find a way to make money while you sleep, you will work until you die." Creating passive income streams is the key to unlocking the shackles of time and location.

Imagine generating income from rental properties, royalties from your bestselling novel, or a successful online business that operates on autopilot. These passive income streams can provide you with the freedom to work when you want, where you want, or not work at all. It's like having your own personal money-making machine while you focus on enjoying life's pleasures.

C. Designing a lifestyle that prioritizes leisure and personal pursuits: Because life is meant to be a grand adventure filled with joy, laughter, and occasional awkward moments.

As the iconic writer Mark Twain humorously noted, "Twenty years from now, you will be more disappointed by the things you didn't do than by the ones you did do. So throw off the bowlines. Sail away from the safe harbor. Catch the trade winds in your sails. Explore. Dream. Discover."

Designing a lifestyle that prioritizes leisure and personal pursuits is about creating a life that brings you joy and fulfillment. It's about embracing those moments of silliness, taking risks, and pursuing activities that ignite your passion.

Imagine waking up each day excited about the possibilities that lie ahead. Whether it's spending time with loved ones, engaging in hobbies, or embarking on wild adventures, your time is yours to design as you please. By escaping the time-for-money trap, you can create a life that's not only financially abundant but also rich in experiences and laughter.

In conclusion, escaping the time-for-money trap is a courageous journey that requires a dash of audacity, a sprinkle of creativity, and a healthy dose of humor. By breaking free from the traditional 9-to-5 job, creating passive income streams, and designing a lifestyle that prioritizes leisure and personal pursuits, you can live life on your terms.

So, my brave reader, it's time to don your cape, spread your wings, and soar into the realm of time and money freedom. Remember, life is too precious to be spent solely trading your time for a paycheck. Embrace the adventure, chase your dreams, and always find humor in the twists and turns of your escapades.

May your journey be filled with laughter, abundance, and a glorious lack of pantyhose-clad hamsters on wheels. Here's to a life where time is your friend, money flows effortlessly, and each day is a delightful romp in the playground of life.

CHAPTER 23: SCALING AND REPLICATING SUCCESS: UNLEASHING YOUR INNER COPYCAT FOR EXPONENTIAL GROWTH

Welcome, my enterprising reader, to a chapter that will take you on a whimsical journey of scaling and replicating success. Picture this: a world where you can multiply your achievements without breaking a sweat or sprouting an extra limb. Sounds intriguing, doesn't it? Well, buckle up and prepare to dive into the art of growth and leverage. Let's unleash your inner copycat and embark on a quest for exponential greatness!

A. Replicating successful strategies and investments for exponential growth: Because why reinvent the wheel when you can hitch a ride on the success train?

As the brilliant scientist and Nobel laureate, Albert Einstein, once said, "The secret to creativity is knowing how to hide your sources." In our case, the secret to growth lies in knowing how to replicate and adapt successful strategies.

Think about it. If someone has already cracked the code and achieved remarkable results, why not follow in their footsteps? Whether it's a tried-and-true investment strategy or a clever marketing campaign, replicating success allows you to fast-track your own growth and avoid reinventing the wheel.

Take inspiration from entrepreneurs like Elon Musk, who scaled the electric vehicle industry by replicating the success of Tesla and applying it to SpaceX. By leveraging existing knowledge and adapting it to new endeavors, you can supercharge your own path to greatness.

B. Scaling businesses and income streams with minimal additional effort: Because a single drop of success can turn into a tidal wave of prosperity.

Imagine having a thriving business that practically runs itself while you sip piña coladas on a tropical beach. Scaling your business means finding ways to increase revenue and expand your operations without adding a mountain of extra work to your plate.

One example of scaling success is Amazon. Jeff Bezos transformed a humble online bookstore into an e-commerce behemoth by continuously adding new products, diversifying their offerings, and leveraging technology to streamline operations. By finding ways to automate and delegate tasks, you can free up your time and energy to focus on strategic growth.

So, my ambitious friend, seek out opportunities to leverage systems, delegate tasks, and multiply your income streams with minimal additional effort. It's like hiring a team of magical clones to do the heavy lifting while you bask in the glory of your empire.

C. Leveraging existing assets and systems for continued success: Because why build from scratch when you can ride the coattails of your previous triumphs?

The legendary investor and philanthropist, Warren Buffett, once remarked, "Someone's sitting in the shade today because someone planted a tree a long time ago." Likewise, you can bask in the shade of your past successes by leveraging existing assets and systems for continued growth.

Consider this: if you've already built a solid foundation, why not capitalize on it? Whether it's a loyal customer base, a robust network, or a well-oiled business process, leveraging your existing assets allows you to compound your success and reach new heights.

Look at Richard Branson, the master of leveraging his brand. He started with a record store and expanded into a conglomerate that includes Virgin Records, Virgin Atlantic, and even Virgin Galactic. By leveraging his existing brand and reputation, he created a network effect that propelled him to even greater success.

So, my resourceful comrade, examine your arsenal of assets and systems. Identify the golden nuggets that have brought you success and find ways to leverage them for future endeavors. It's like unlocking a secret vault of opportunities that will catapult you to new dimensions of achievement.

In conclusion, scaling and replicating success is not about copying blindly or chasing after fleeting trends. It's about strategically adapting proven strategies, scaling businesses and income streams, and leveraging existing assets and systems to create a virtuous cycle of growth.

As the great Winston Churchill once said, "To improve is to change; to be perfect is to change often." Embrace change, my tenacious friend, and let it fuel your journey towards exponential growth. Scaling and replicating success is your ticket to a life where achievements snowball, and the sky's the limit.

So go forth, dear reader, armed with the knowledge and wit acquired from this chapter, and conquer the world with your scaled-up empire. Just remember to save a piña colada for me when you reach that tropical beach. Cheers to your magnificent replication of success!

CHAPTER 24: LIVING THE LAZY MILLIONAIRE LIFESTYLE: EMBRACE YOUR INNER COUCH POTATO AND PROSPER!

Welcome, my fellow lazy enthusiasts, to a chapter that will transform your perspective on success and redefine what it means to live the good life. Picture this: reclining on your plush sofa, remote in hand, surrounded by all the trappings of luxury. Sounds like a dream, doesn't it? Well, get ready to turn that dream into a reality as we delve into the art of living the lazy millionaire lifestyle!

A. Embracing the freedom and abundance that comes with being a lazy millionaire: Because life is too short to spend it toiling away like a hamster on a wheel.

Imagine waking up when your body feels like it, not when the alarm clock dictates. Imagine having the freedom to pursue your passions, indulge in leisurely activities, and travel the world without a care in the world. As the wise philosopher Ferris Bueller once said, "Life moves pretty fast. If you don't stop and look around once in a while, you could miss it."

Being a lazy millionaire means breaking free from the shackles of traditional work and embracing a life of abundance and freedom. It's about creating passive income streams that work tirelessly for you, allowing you to enjoy the fruits of your labor while lounging in your favorite pajamas.

Take inspiration from successful lazy millionaires like Tim Ferriss, who authored "The 4-Hour Workweek" and built a lifestyle business that generates income with minimal effort. By focusing on efficiency and leveraging the power of automation, he embraced the lazy millionaire mindset and empowered others to do the same.

B. Enjoying leisure time and pursuing passions without financial worries: Because life's too short to be a workaholic or worry about bills.

Now, my fellow leisure enthusiasts, let's talk about the sweet nectar of life: leisure time. As the legendary author Mark Twain once quipped, "The best way to cheer yourself is to try to cheer someone else up." And what better way to cheer yourself up than by pursuing your passions and enjoying life's pleasures without the burden of financial worries?

Being a lazy millionaire means having the financial freedom to indulge in activities that bring you joy. Whether it's traveling to exotic destinations, engaging in hobbies that light your soul on fire, or simply spending quality time with loved ones, the lazy millionaire lifestyle allows you to savor life's exquisite moments.

Let's not forget about the power of philanthropy, my benevolent friend. As a lazy millionaire, you have the opportunity to make a positive impact on the world. Take a page from the book of philanthropic magnate Bill Gates, who once said, "The moral imperative is to give, not just to give back, but to give forward." Use your wealth to support causes that align with your values and inspire others to embrace a life of abundance and generosity.

C. Inspiring others to embrace a new definition of success: Because the lazy millionaire lifestyle is contagious and meant to be shared.

As you embark on your lazy millionaire journey, my charismatic friend, remember the power of influence. Your newfound freedom and abundance can inspire others to question the conventional definition of success and pursue their own lazy millionaire dreams.

Look to successful lazy millionaires like Richard Branson, who founded the Virgin Group and has become an icon of entrepreneurship and adventurous living. His audacious spirit and zest for life have inspired countless individuals to think outside the box and strive for a life of fulfillment and leisure.

Share your story, my lazy millionaire extraordinaire. Spread the gospel of freedom and abundance. Encourage others to break free from the chains of traditional work and embrace a life where they can pursue their passions and revel in leisure without financial worries.

In conclusion, living the lazy millionaire lifestyle is not just about lounging around in your silk bathrobe or binging on your favorite Netflix series (although those are delightful perks). It's about embracing the freedom, abundance, and joy that come with financial success, while inspiring others to redefine their own path to fulfillment.

So, my fellow lazy millionaires, go forth and conquer the world with your laid-back charm and financial prowess. Remember the words of the indomitable Oscar Wilde, who said, "To live is the rarest thing in the world. Most people exist, that is all." Embrace the lazy millionaire lifestyle and truly live!

May your days be filled with leisure, laughter, and a generous sprinkling of laziness. Onward to the land of abundance and slothful delight!

CHAPTER 25: GIVING BACK AND MAKING A DIFFERENCE: BECAUSE SHARING THE WEALTH IS JUST MORE FUN

Ah, my generous friend, welcome to a chapter that will warm your heart and tickle your funny bone as we explore the delightful world of giving back and making a difference. Prepare to don your cape of philanthropy and unleash your inner superhero as we delve into the power of using wealth and influence for the greater good. Let's dive in and discover how you can leave a positive mark on the world!

A. Using wealth and influence to make a positive impact on the world: Because being a lazy millionaire is not just about lounging on a yacht with a drink in hand.

As a lazy millionaire, you possess a superpower that can change lives and transform communities. With great wealth comes great responsibility, as the iconic Uncle Ben from Spider-Man famously said, "With great power comes great responsibility."

Think of legendary figures like Warren Buffett, the "Oracle of Omaha," who uses his wealth and influence to tackle global issues. Through his charitable foundation, Buffett has pledged to donate 99% of his fortune to causes such as poverty alleviation and education. He understood that true fulfillment comes from making a positive impact on the lives of others.

But fear not, my generous friend, you don't need to be a billionaire to make a difference. Even small acts of kindness and generosity can have a profound impact. Whether it's donating to a local charity, volunteering your time and skills, or advocating for causes you believe in, every effort counts.

B. Supporting charitable causes and philanthropic endeavors: Because it's more fun to be a part of the solution than to watch the world go down the drain.

Now, let's delve into the exciting world of supporting charitable causes and philanthropic endeavors. It's time to put on your fundraising hat and get ready to make it rain... donations, that is!

Explore the causes that resonate with you, my charitable connoisseur. Whether it's education, healthcare, environmental conservation, or social justice, there are countless organizations and initiatives in need of your support. As the wise and witty Maya Angelou once said, "I have found that among its other benefits, giving liberates the soul of the giver."

Consider joining forces with other lazy millionaires, forming a league of extraordinary philanthropists. Together, you can pool your resources and create even greater impact. Just imagine the power of your collective wealth and influence! It's like the Avengers, but with tuxedos and champagne instead of spandex and superpowers.

C. Leveraging your resources to create a better future for others: Because it's not just about writing a check, it's about making a lasting impact.

Now, my resourceful changemaker, let's talk about the importance of leveraging your resources to create a better future for others. It's time to channel your inner Tony Stark and use your ingenuity to tackle societal challenges.

Think beyond traditional forms of giving, my innovative friend. Consider using your wealth and influence to invest in social enterprises and startups that address pressing issues. By providing financial support and mentorship, you can help these ventures grow and create sustainable solutions.

Take inspiration from remarkable individuals like Elon Musk, the eccentric genius behind companies like Tesla and SpaceX. Musk's vision extends far beyond creating electric cars and colonizing Mars. He actively seeks to address global problems such as climate change and renewable energy. Through initiatives like the SolarCity project, he is transforming the way we think about energy consumption.

But let's not forget the power of your time and expertise, my knowledgeable philanthropist. By sharing your skills and knowledge, you can empower others and spark meaningful change. Consider mentoring aspiring entrepreneurs, teaching financial literacy, or participating in community development programs. Your guidance and support can be a catalyst for success.

As you embark on your philanthropic journey, remember the words of the iconic Mahatma Gandhi: "The best way to find yourself is to lose yourself in the service of others." In giving back, you not only uplift others but also find a deeper sense of purpose and fulfillment.

So, my generous friend, let your heart guide you as you navigate the world of philanthropy. Use your wealth, influence, and wit to make a positive impact. Together, let's create a future where laziness and generosity go hand in hand, making the world a better place—one lazy millionaire at a time.

CHAPTER 26: OVERCOMING CHALLENGES ON THE PATH TO LAZINESS: BECAUSE EVEN LAZY MILLIONAIRES HAVE THEIR MOMENTS

Welcome, my fellow lazy millionaire, to a chapter filled with wit, humor, and practical wisdom as we navigate the challenges on our path to laziness. Fear not, for even in the realm of laziness, obstacles may arise, but with a little creativity and resilience, we shall overcome. So, let's roll up our sleeves... or better yet, roll over in our cozy hammocks, as we explore the art of overcoming challenges on the path to laziness.

A. Addressing common challenges and obstacles faced by lazy millionaires: Because even the laziest among us can stumble upon a hurdle or two.

Ah, the challenges of the lazy millionaire life! From rising taxes to unexpected market fluctuations, we must navigate a few bumps on our path to eternal leisure. But fret not, my friend, for we shall conquer these challenges with a mischievous smile on our faces.

One common challenge we face is the temptation to deviate from our lazy ways. It's all too easy to be enticed by shiny new investment opportunities or succumb to the siren call of busywork. But remember the wise words of the legendary Albert Einstein: "The definition of genius is taking the complex and making it simple." So, let us resist the urge to complicate our lives and stay true to our lazy, yet brilliant, selves.

Another challenge we encounter is the ever-changing economic landscape. Markets fluctuate, trends come and go, and financial tides can turn in an instant. However, as the cunning investor Warren Buffett once said, "The stock market is a device for transferring money from the impatient to the patient." So, let us stay patient, ride the waves, and trust in the power of our well-diversified, lazily managed portfolios.

B. Developing resilience and adapting to changing circumstances: Because life has a funny way of testing our laziness, and we shall rise to the occasion.

Ah, my resilient comrade, the path to laziness may not always be smooth sailing. But fear not, for we shall adapt and conquer. Life may throw curveballs at us, but we shall lazily swing at them and hit them out of the park.

In times of adversity, let us draw inspiration from the indomitable spirit of successful individuals who have faced their fair share of challenges. Take the story of J.K. Rowling, the brilliant mind behind the Harry Potter series. Before her success, she faced rejection after rejection. But she persevered, believing in the power of her story. And as Dumbledore wisely said, "Happiness can be found even in the darkest of times if one only remembers to turn on the light." So, my resilient friend, let us turn on the light and navigate the challenges with a twinkle in our eye.

Adaptability is our secret weapon, dear lazy millionaire. Just like the chameleon changes its colors to blend into its surroundings, we must adapt our strategies to the changing circumstances. Embrace new technologies, seize emerging opportunities, and remember that even the laziest of us can learn new tricks. As the great Steve Jobs once quipped, "Innovation distinguishes between a leader and a follower." So, let us be leaders in our laziness, always ready to embrace the winds of change.

C. Finding creative solutions to maintain and grow your wealth: Because laziness is not just about preserving what we have, but also about creating a legacy of leisure.

Ah, the pursuit of laziness requires a touch of ingenuity and a dash of creativity. When faced with challenges, my resourceful friend, let us summon the power of our brilliant minds to find unconventional solutions.

In the face of increasing taxes, seek the advice of shrewd accountants and tax strategists who can help us navigate the complex web of regulations. Remember the words of Benjamin Franklin: "In this world, nothing can be said to be certain, except death and taxes." But with proper planning, we can minimize the impact of taxes and maximize our lazy enjoyment.

To protect our wealth from the whims of the market, consider diversifying into alternative assets that provide stability and passive income. Real estate, for example, has been a tried and true avenue for lazy millionaires to preserve and grow their wealth. As the renowned businessman Andrew Carnegie once said, "Ninety percent of all millionaires become so through owning real estate." So, let us follow in the footsteps of the real estate moguls and create a fortress of laziness with our diverse and carefully curated portfolio.

And finally, my creative companion, let us not forget the power of collaboration. Seek the wisdom and advice of fellow lazy millionaires, share insights, and pool resources. Together, we can conquer any challenge that comes our way. As the great Henry

Ford once said, "Coming together is a beginning, staying together is progress, and working together is success." So, let us come together in our pursuit of ultimate laziness and create a network of indolent brilliance.

In conclusion, dear lazy millionaire, challenges may arise on our path to laziness, but with resilience, adaptability, and creative solutions, we shall prevail. Remember, even the most ingenious among us face hurdles, but it is our ability to overcome them that sets us apart. So, my fellow connoisseur of leisure, let us embrace the challenges as opportunities for growth and refinement. Together, we shall rise above, with a smile on our faces and a cocktail in our hand, for we are the embodiment of the lazy millionaire spirit.

And as we navigate these challenges, let us not forget the wise words of Mark Twain: "The secret of getting ahead is getting started. The secret of getting started is breaking your complex overwhelming tasks into small manageable tasks, and then starting on the first one." So, my friend, let us break down the challenges, lazily tackle them one by one, and continue on our journey to a life of abundance and leisure.

CHAPTER 27: CONTINUOUS LEARNING AND ADAPTATION: BECAUSE EVEN LAZY MILLIONAIRES NEED TO KEEP THEIR MINDS SHARP

Welcome, my fellow aficionados of laziness, to a chapter that celebrates the art of continuous learning and adaptation. Yes, even in the realm of ultimate laziness, we must exercise our minds to stay ahead of the game. So, grab your favorite reading glasses and prepare to embark on a journey of intellectual stimulation, all while maintaining our laid-back and humorous demeanor.

A. Embracing a growth mindset and committing to lifelong learning: Because a lazy mind is a terrible thing to waste.

Ah, the beauty of a growth mindset, my friend. It is the foundation upon which we build our lazy empires. As the brilliant psychologist Carol Dweck once said, "In a growth mindset, challenges are seen as opportunities for growth and effort is the path to mastery." So, let us adopt this mindset and embrace the joy of continuous learning.

Remember the story of Thomas Edison and his quest to invent the light bulb? He famously said, "I have not failed. I've just found 10,000 ways that won't work." This mindset of seeing failures as stepping stones to success is the key to our lazy intellectual evolution. So, let us not be discouraged by setbacks but rather see them as valuable lessons on our journey to laziness.

Lifelong learning doesn't have to be a tedious affair, my dear lazy millionaire. Explore subjects that pique your interest, whether it's the history of bubble wrap or the psychology of cat videos. As the great Albert Einstein once quipped, "I have no special talents. I am only passionately curious." So, let your curiosity guide you, and delve into the vast ocean of knowledge, all from the comfort of your hammock.

B. Staying updated on industry trends and market opportunities: Because even lazy millionaires need to know where the money flows.

Ah, my wise and informed companion, staying updated on industry trends and market opportunities is the key to maintaining our lazy wealth. But fear not, for we shall approach this task with the wit and humor befitting our esteemed status.

In today's fast-paced world, information flows like a lazy river. Embrace the power of technology and leverage the countless resources available at your fingertips. Online publications, industry forums, and social media channels are treasure troves of information, just waiting to be lazily explored. Remember the words of the witty Oscar Wilde: "I never travel without my diary. One should always have something sensational to read on the train." So, let us indulge in sensational industry news as we recline in our private jets, sipping champagne.

Be mindful of the trends and shifts in the market, my lazy friend. Just as the winds change direction, so too do the tides of opportunity. Study the success stories of industry leaders, learn from their strategies, and adapt them to fit your own lazily brilliant endeavors. As the legendary Warren Buffett once said, "The best investment you can make is in yourself." So, invest in your knowledge, stay informed, and ride the waves of opportunity with your signature lazy finesse.

C. Adapting your strategies to changing economic landscapes: Because even the laziest of millionaires must adjust their sails to the winds of change.

Ah, my adaptable comrade, the economic landscape is ever-changing, and we must be prepared to adjust our strategies accordingly. But fear not, for we shall approach this task with the grace and humor that defines our lazy spirit.

Consider the story of Blockbuster, once a titan of the entertainment industry. They failed to adapt to the rise of streaming services and fell into the pit of obsolescence. As the wise Charles Darwin said, "It is not the strongest of the species that survives, nor the most intelligent; it is the one most adaptable to change." So, let us not be like Blockbuster but rather embrace change with open arms and a lazy smile.

Keep an eye on emerging technologies and disruptive innovations that have the potential to transform industries. The rise of artificial intelligence, blockchain, and virtual reality are not just buzzwords but opportunities for us to lazily ride the wave of progress. As the innovative Elon Musk once said, "The first step is to establish that something is possible; then probability will occur." So, let us establish the possibilities, my friend, and let probability work its magic while we recline on our futuristic bean bags.

In conclusion, my fellow lazy learners, the path to ultimate laziness requires a commitment to continuous learning and adaptation. Embrace a growth mindset, stay updated on industry trends, and adapt your strategies to the ever-changing economic landscape. Remember, even the laziest of millionaires must exercise their minds to keep their wealth growing. So, let us embark on this journey of intellectual stimulation, all while maintaining our signature wit and humor. And as the great Winston Churchill once said, "To improve is to change; to be perfect is to change often." So, let us strive for perfection in our laziness by continuously learning and adapting to the world around us.

CHAPTER 28: BALANCING LAZINESS AND PRODUCTIVITY: FINDING THE SWEET SPOT BETWEEN WORK AND PLAY

Welcome, my fellow masters of laziness and productivity, to a chapter that celebrates the delicate dance of finding the optimal balance between laziness and getting things done. In this chapter, we shall explore the art of being effortlessly efficient, all while maintaining our trademark wit and humor. So, put on your thinking caps (or not, if you prefer), and let us embark on this journey of harmonizing work and play.

A. Finding the optimal balance between laziness and productivity: The pursuit of the perfect equilibrium.

Ah, the eternal quest for the sweet spot between laziness and productivity. It's like finding the mythical unicorn that brings you coffee in bed. But fear not, my fellow lazy achievers, for we shall unravel this enigma with our trademark wit and wisdom.

As the great writer Mark Twain once said, "The secret of getting ahead is getting started. The secret of getting started is breaking your complex, overwhelming tasks into small manageable tasks, and then starting on the first one." So, let us break down our seemingly daunting tasks into bite-sized nuggets of laziness. By focusing on one small task at a time, we can maintain our laziness while gradually making progress toward our goals.

However, let us not fall into the trap of overworking ourselves, my dear lazy comrades. Remember the wise words of the legendary Albert Einstein: "If a cluttered desk is a sign of a cluttered mind, of what, then, is an empty desk a sign?" So, embrace the power of laziness and give yourself permission to take breaks, relax, and indulge in activities that bring you joy. It is in these moments of leisure that our creative juices flow and our productivity skyrockets.

B. Harnessing the power of focused effort and decision-making: Laziness with a purpose.

Ah, the paradox of laziness and focused effort. It's like sipping a piña colada while juggling flaming torches. But fear not, for we shall master this tightrope act with the grace and humor that defines us.

When it comes to focused effort, my lazy accomplice, remember the wise words of the great basketball player Michael Jordan: "Obstacles don't have to stop you. If you run into a wall, don't turn around and give up. Figure out how to climb it, go through it, or work around it." So, channel your inner Jordan and approach your tasks with laser-like focus. Allocate specific time blocks for deep work, free from distractions, and witness your productivity soar to new lazy heights.

Now, let us delve into the realm of decision-making, my wise and witty companion. As the iconic Steve Jobs once said, "Deciding what not to do is as important as deciding what to do." So, be selective in your pursuits, my lazy millionaire friend. Prioritize tasks that align with your goals and values, and delegate or eliminate the rest. This way, you can optimize your time and energy for activities that truly matter, all while basking in the glory of your laziness.

C. Maximizing results while minimizing unnecessary work: The lazy path to efficiency.

Ah, the art of maximizing results with minimal effort. It's like finding a shortcut that leads to a treasure trove of success. But fear not, for we shall navigate this labyrinth of efficiency with the wit and humor that define our lazy spirit.

Automation, my ingenious accomplice, is the secret weapon of the lazy millionaire. As the brilliant inventor Nikola Tesla once said, "The desire that guides me in all I do is the desire to harness the forces of nature to the service of mankind." So, let us harness the forces of automation to our advantage. Identify repetitive tasks that can be automated, whether it's through software, outsourcing, or delegating to capable assistants. By freeing ourselves from mundane and time-consuming activities, we can focus on the pursuits that truly bring us joy and wealth.

Furthermore, my fellow lazy achievers, embrace the power of leverage. As the legendary investor Warren Buffett once said, "If you don't find a way to make money while you sleep, you will work until you die." So, seek opportunities to leverage your time, money, and resources. Invest in income-generating assets such as real estate, stocks, or businesses that can generate passive income streams. This way, you can enjoy the fruits of your laziness while your money works hard for you.

In conclusion, my witty and wise companion, balancing laziness and productivity is an art that requires finesse, focus, and a dash of humor. Find the optimal equilibrium between work and play, harness the power of focused effort and decision-making, and maximize results while minimizing unnecessary work. Remember, we are lazy millionaires, and our quest for success is defined by effortless efficiency and joyful pursuits. So, let us dance on the fine line between laziness and productivity, all while wearing our slippers of success. And as the great Charlie Chaplin once said, "A day without laughter is a day wasted." So, my friend, let us laugh, be lazy, and conquer the world in our own delightfully unique way.

CHAPTER 29: CULTIVATING FINANCIAL INDEPENDENCE FOR GENERATIONS: LAZY MILLIONAIRE'S GUIDE TO LEAVING A LEGACY

Welcome, fellow lazy millionaires, to a chapter dedicated to the noble pursuit of cultivating financial independence for generations to come. In this chapter, we shall explore the art of passing down wealth, knowledge, and the lazy millionaire mindset to our loved ones, all while maintaining our signature wit and humor. So, grab your monocles and top hats, my dear friends, and let us embark on this journey of creating a lasting legacy of financial freedom and abundance.

A. Passing down wealth and knowledge to future generations: The lazy millionaire's inheritance strategy.

Ah, the joy of sharing the spoils of our lazy success with those we hold dear. As the wise Greek philosopher Aristotle once said, "The whole is greater than the sum of its parts." So, let us explore how we can pass down our wealth and wisdom to future generations, creating a legacy that extends far beyond our own lifetime.

The first step, my dear inheritors of laziness, is to establish a solid estate plan. Consult with legal and financial experts to create a comprehensive will, trust, and other mechanisms that ensure a smooth transition of your assets. By taking care of the logistical aspects, you can focus on imparting the lazy millionaire mindset and guiding principles to your successors.

Now, let us turn our attention to the aspect of knowledge transfer. As the renowned scientist Isaac Newton once said, "If I have seen further, it is by standing on the shoulders of giants." Share your experiences, lessons learned, and the secrets of your lazy millionaire success with the next generation. Host family meetings, create educational resources, and encourage open discussions about money, investing, and the pursuit of happiness. By equipping your loved ones with the knowledge and mindset necessary for lazy prosperity, you ensure that your legacy lives on.

B. Educating and empowering loved ones to become lazy millionaires: The gift of knowledge and freedom.

Ah, the joy of empowering our loved ones to follow in our lazy footsteps. As the wise and whimsical Willy Wonka once said, "We are the music-makers, and we are the dreamers of dreams." Let us be the dreamers of a future where our loved ones can embrace the lazy millionaire lifestyle with confidence and ease.

Education, my wise and witty companion, is the key to unlocking the lazy millionaire potential in our successors. Encourage a culture of continuous learning and personal growth within your family. Provide resources, recommend books, and share your favorite podcasts or TED Talks that inspire and educate on topics such as entrepreneurship, investing, and financial independence.

Furthermore, instill in your loved ones the importance of embracing their passions and pursuing work that brings them joy.

As the iconic Steve Jobs once said, "Your work is going to fill a large part of your life, and the only way to be truly satisfied is to do what you believe is great work." Encourage them to find their unique path to lazy success, whether it be through entrepreneurship, creative endeavors, or investing in income-generating assets.

C. Ensuring a legacy of financial freedom and abundance: Lazy millionaires, leaving their mark.

Ah, the satisfaction of knowing that our lazy legacy will endure for generations to come. As the brilliant inventor Thomas Edison once said, "I have not failed. I've just found 10,000 ways that won't work." Let us ensure that our legacy of financial freedom and abundance stands the test of time.

One way to preserve your lazy millionaire legacy is by establishing a family foundation or charitable trust. As your wealth grows, consider allocating a portion of it to support causes that align with your values. Not only does this leave a lasting impact on society, but it also instills in your successors the importance of giving back. As the philanthropist Melinda Gates once said, "When you lift up women, you lift up humanity." So, let us lift up the world with our lazy generosity.

Finally, my witty and wise companion, do not underestimate the power of storytelling. Share the stories of your lazy millionaire journey with your family. Narrate the triumphs, the failures, and the valuable lessons learned along the way. Stories have the unique ability to inspire, educate, and connect generations. As the great Maya Angelou once said, "I've learned that people will forget what you said, people will forget what you did, but people will never forget how you made them feel." So, let us make our loved ones feel the magic and possibility that comes with being a lazy millionaire.

In conclusion, my fellow lazy visionaries, cultivating financial independence for generations is not just about money and assets; it is about imparting the mindset, values, and knowledge that have brought us lazy success. By passing down our wealth and wisdom, educating and empowering our loved ones, and ensuring a legacy of financial freedom and abundance, we create a future where laziness and prosperity go hand in hand. So, let us be the architects of a lazy dynasty, where each generation builds upon the foundation laid by their lazy predecessors. And as we revel in the joy of knowing that our legacy will endure, let us raise our glasses and toast to a future filled with lazy millionaires who continue to inspire and delight the world. Cheers!

CHAPTER 30: CONCLUSION: LAZY MILLIONAIRE - THE FINAL CURTAIN CALL

Ah, dear readers, we have reached the grand finale of our lazy millionaire escapade. It is time to tie up the loose ends, recap the key concepts, and bid farewell with a final dose of wit and wisdom. So, without further ado, let us embark on this concluding chapter and bring our journey to a satisfying close.

A. Summarizing the key concepts and strategies discussed throughout the book: A lazy millionaire's greatest hits.

Oh, the sweet symphony of laziness and wealth. As we reflect on the chapters past, let us highlight the key concepts and strategies that have graced the pages of this magnificent tome.

Embracing the Power of Laziness: Laziness is not a flaw; it is a virtue. By embracing laziness, we free ourselves from the shackles of conventional thinking and discover innovative ways to achieve financial success.

Creating Streams of Passive Income: Ah, the allure of passive income, where money flows effortlessly into our pockets like a gentle stream. From real estate investments to dividend-paying stocks and online businesses, we have explored various avenues to generate lazy income.

Mastering the Art of Automation: The lazy millionaire's secret weapon, automation, saves us time, effort, and headaches. From automated investment contributions to outsourcing mundane tasks, we have harnessed the power of technology and delegation to maximize our lazy potential.

Diversifying with Delight: Ah, the thrill of diversification, like a delicious buffet for our lazy portfolios. We have explored different asset classes, from stocks and bonds to cryptocurrencies and alternative investments, to ensure our wealth is well-protected and primed for growth.

Cultivating a Lazy Millionaire Mindset: Success begins in the mind, dear readers. We have nurtured a mindset of abundance, resilience, and creativity. By adopting a growth mindset and surrounding ourselves with positive influences, we have conquered the hurdles on our lazy path to wealth.

B. Reinforcing the idea that laziness can be a pathway to financial success: The lazy millionaire's anthem.

Now, let us address the skeptics, the naysayers who dare question the legitimacy of our lazy pursuits. As the brilliant Albert Einstein once said, "Genius is 1% talent and 99% percent hard work." Well, we, my dear friends, are the 1% of genius who understand that laziness can be the catalyst for financial success.

Throughout history, we have seen countless examples of lazy millionaires who have defied societal norms and carved their own path to prosperity. Take the visionary Elon Musk, who has revolutionized the electric vehicle industry while lounging in his favorite armchair. Or the indomitable Oprah Winfrey, whose empire was built on her ability to inspire and entertain, all from the comfort of her talk show stage.

Laziness, when harnessed with intention and purpose, becomes a superpower. It allows us to conserve our energy for the truly important tasks, to delegate and automate, and to focus on the activities that bring us joy and fulfillment. As the great comedian and actor Jim Carrey once said, "I think everybody should get rich and famous and do everything they ever dreamed of so they can see that it's not the answer." Laziness is our guiding light, reminding us to prioritize what truly matters in life.

C. Encouraging readers to take action and embark on their own lazy millionaire journey: The final call to action.

Ah, dear readers, we have journeyed together through the realms of laziness and wealth, savoring the flavors of success and reveling in the joy of a life well-lived. But our journey does not end here. Nay, it is but the beginning for you, my dear companion.

I implore you, do not let the wisdom and inspiration gained from these pages go to waste. Take action, my friend, and embark on your own lazy millionaire journey. Embrace the principles we have explored, adapt them to your unique circumstances, and craft your own path to lazy riches.

Remember the tale of the lazy entrepreneur who turned a passion for napping into a thriving mattress empire? Or the story of the indolent investor who built an empire by carefully selecting investments while lounging in a hammock? These stories are not mere fantasies; they are living proof that laziness can be the catalyst for extraordinary success.

So, my dear reader, as we bid adieu to this whimsical adventure, I leave you with the words of the iconic Walt Disney: "All our dreams can come true if we have the courage to pursue them." Summon your lazy courage, my friend, and embark on your own lazy millionaire odyssey. The world awaits your indolent brilliance!

And with that, we draw the final curtain on this captivating journey. It has been an honor to be your witty and wise companion, guiding you through the realms of laziness and wealth. May your days be filled with joy, abundance, and the sweet satisfaction of achieving greatness with minimal effort. Farewell, dear reader, and may you forever bask in the glory of your lazy millionaire lifestyle. Until we meet again!